GERANIUM

Reaktion's Botanical series is the first of its kind, integrating horticultural and botanical writing with a broader account of the cultural and social impact of trees, plants and flowers. Accessibly written yet encompassing the latest scholarship, each title features around 100 fine images.

Published

Oak Peter Young
Geranium Kasia Boddy

Forthcoming
Lily, Yew, Pine, Willow, Palm, Orchid and others

Geranium

Kasia Boddy

REAKTION BOOKS

For Ali Smith, who likes the plants, and for Andrew Boddy,
who likes the history that surrounds them

Published by
REAKTION BOOKS LTD
33 Great Sutton Street
London EC1V ODX, UK

www.reaktionbooks.co.uk

First published 2013

Printed and bound in China by C&C Offset Printing Co., Ltd

British Library Cataloguing in Publication Data
Boddy, Kasia.
Geranium. – (Botanical)
1. Pelargoniums. 2. Pelargoniums – History.
I. Title II. Series
635.9'3379-DC23

ISBN 978 1 78023 048 1

Contents

✦✦✦

SCARLET GERANIUM

Scarlet Zonal Pelargonium. Chromolithograph by F. Edward Hulme.

Introduction

✿❀✿

In 1947, a teenaged Shirley Temple starred in *Honeymoon*, a Hollywood comedy about a 'flighty little subdeb' from the Midwest who, after a bump on the head, fancies herself in love with a suave diplomat (Franchot Tone) rather than her boy-next-door fiancé (Guy Madison).[1] We doubt that Shirley and Franchot are ever going to make a pair, especially when she breaks into song to declare her taste in flowers.

> Some ladies love to get orchids,
> Or roses with stems a mile long,
> Some girls prefer a gardenia,
> Camellias might ring the gong,
> Or sometimes they like an old fashioned
>   bouquet,
> A quaint little nosegay on Valentine's Day.
> But I must disagree,
> These species are not for me.
>
> I love geraniums,
> Bright, red geraniums,
>
> And ev'rytime I see one
> I always think of you.[2]

Shirley Temple, Franchot Tone and Guy Madison in *Honeymoon* (1947). Film still.

Of course it's not sophisticated Franchot who resembles a bright red geranium, but jovially hapless Guy. The romantic entanglement resolves when she manages to match man to flower.

Like Shirley, many of us love bright red geraniums and, even if we don't, we can't escape them. Walk down any street in Birmingham, Berne, Brisbane, Berkeley or Bangalore and you'll see a geranium or two: trailing from a window box or nestled among petunias in a pub hanging-basket; perched in its pot on a fire-escape or straining for sunlight behind an office blind; or dazzling, en masse, in front of the local museum. Do the geraniums draw attention to statues of great men or, as Wallace Stevens worried, do their memorials simply become 'a setting for geraniums'?[3]

The global presence of the bright red geranium is due to the fact that, despite its origins in a very specific climate, it has proved adaptable to so many others. Admirers point out the plant's 'extreme good nature', the fact that 'it never seems to think that it has any special rights or requirements'.

It is not fussy about its food, it had no distinctive pest or disease . . . it is not particular about its neighbours; it has not even a 'season', during which it monopolizes attention by its extravagant glory and after which it retires and leaves its foliage *de trop*. . . . Given any chance at all, anywhere, no matter how grudgingly, it makes itself at home and settles down to its perennial occupation.[4]

Lenin among a bed of red geraniums in front of Lenin Memorial Museum at the Smolny Institute, St Petersburg.

A wall covered in geranium pots in Cordoba, Andalucia, for the Festival de los Patios.

It's no surprise that when the poet Ed Dorn was looking for a flower to represent the 'cherishable common' he turned to the scarlet geranium.[5]

Of course the bright red geranium isn't, botanically speaking, a *Geranium* at all; in fact it's probably a *Pelargonium x hortorum*. Specialists can get very shirty when people get this wrong – and they often do.

The confusion arose in the seventeenth century when the first pelargoniums were brought from southern Africa to Europe. Like the hardy perennials that Europeans knew as geraniums, these tender shrubs had flowers of five petals and therefore five seedpods, each of which resembled a crane's elongated head and beak.[6] But it didn't take botanists long to observe that, apart from their seed-heads, geraniums and pelargoniums are really very different. Geraniums have regular flowers, in most cases consisting of five identical petals, and ten to fifteen pollen-producing stamens. Pelargoniums have irregular flowers – the two upper petals differing from the lower three in size, shape and markings – with a nectar spur and only two to seven pollen-producing stamens. Unlike pelargoniums, geraniums are never red.

These morphological differences were hard to miss and in 1732, the Oxford botanist Johann Jakob Dillenius suggested that 'if anyone wishes to make a new genus of these geraniums which have unequal or irregular flowers . . . they be called after the Greek word for a stork – pelargonium – just as we called geraniums from the crane.'[7] The distinction might have caught on at this point had it not been decisively rejected just a few years later by the most influential botanist of the era, Linnaeus. Linnaeus's *Species Plantarum* (1753) was the ground-breaking work that established binominal nomenclature for seed plants – that is, giving the name of the species in a Latin binomial, the genus followed by a single epithet. *Pelargonium peltatum*, then, is the pelargonium with shield-shaped leaves, although now more generally known as ivy-leaved. Linnaeus included twenty pelargoniums in his book, but neither he nor his followers accepted that the observable differences from geraniums and erodiums were sufficient to justify a generic division.[8]

The man credited as the 'author' of *Pelargonium*, for finally establishing its distinctiveness, was Charles-Louis L'Héritier, a French aristocrat and keen amateur botanist. While the late eighteenth century might have been the best of times to be a botanist, it was certainly the worst of times to be a French aristocrat. In 1787 and 1788, L'Héritier paid little attention to mounting revolutionary fervour and instead prepared and circulated a series of plant descriptions and illustrations, most by Pierre-Joseph Redouté, from a projected magnum opus on the Geraniaceae family. Rather than complete his 'Compendium Generalogium', however, L'Héritier went to London to assist William Aiton, who was compiling the first catalogue of plants at Kew Gardens. He returned to Paris but lost his job and much of his private fortune and could no longer afford to publish his botanical works. In 1800 he was assassinated and only some of his work was later recovered.[9] Today L'Héritier is recognized for describing, in his unpublished manuscript and in Aiton's *Hortus Kewensis*, 21 distinct species of *Pelargonium* and, more importantly, for establishing the botanical distinction between the genera once and for all.

But maintaining that distinction wasn't so simple. By this time, 'African geraniums' had been around for 150 years and British commercial growers and gardeners were reluctant to give up the familiar name.[10] (There was less fuss in other European countries, which came later to the plants.) The standoff between botanists and horticulturalists was exemplified by the nurseryman Henry Andrews's pointedly titled *Geraniums* (1805–6). Andrews was convinced that 'the splitting of Linnaeus's genus' was a bad idea, claiming that if the new generic divisions were adopted, 'the approach of botanic science would be so choked up with ill-shaped, useless lumber that, like a castle in a fairy tale, guarded by hideous dwarfs, none but a botanic Quixote would attempt investigation.'[11] Since then, the salesman's dislike of anything that might prove off-putting to his customers has been echoed in the poet's 'almost routine' expression of distrust for a rival language.[12] Wordsworth famously caricatured 'the Man of Science', who would 'peep and botanize upon his mother's grave', while Emerson

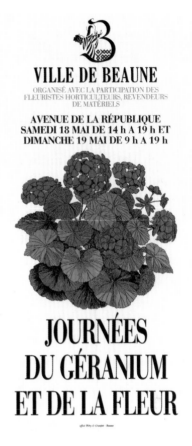

Journées du
Géranium, Ville
de Beune. A poster
celebrating geraniums
in Burgundy.

VILLE DE BEAUNE

ORGANISÉ AVEC LA PARTICIPATION DES
FLEURISTES HORTICULTEURS, REVENDEURS
DE MATÉRIELS

**AVENUE DE LA RÉPUBLIQUE
SAMEDI 18 MAI DE 14 h A 19 h ET
DIMANCHE 19 MAI DE 9 h A 19 h**

**JOURNÉES
DU GÉRANIUM
ET DE LA FLEUR**

dismissed 'young scholars' who 'love not the flower they pluck, and know it not'.[13] Love was what poetry offered. While the botanist observes the distinctions between plants, 'for the sake of swelling his herbarium', sneered John Ruskin, the poet looks in order to 'render them vehicles of expression and emotion.'[14] But if *Pelargonium* was certainly out in the expressive stakes, some even disliked the common name 'geranium'. Although a 'soft and elegant' word, it too was regrettably Greek and, moreover, descriptive of the plant's seedhead. 'What a reason for naming the *flower!*' complained Leigh Hunt, 'as if the fruit were anything in comparison, or any one cared about it . . . It would be better for the world at large to invent joyous and beautiful names for these images of joy.'[15]

Nearly two hundred years later, the battle of nomenclature rumbles on, and passions haven't cooled. There are certainly inconsistencies. It is not uncommon to find, in the same book or garden centre, 'pelargonium' being applied to scented-leaved or Regal varieties, with 'geranium' reserved for bedding plants – 'Zonal pelargoniums!' exclaimed a horrified Derek Jarman, 'Geraniums remain for me geraniums.'[16] Derek Clifford tried to circumvent the matter with the confusingly titled *Pelargoniums, Including the Popular 'Geranium'*, while most other writers have resorted to introductory formulations such as '"geraniums" (pelargoniums, correctly)'.[17] Specialists are sterner. Diana Miller maintains 'there can be no excuse today for the incorrect use of the name "Geranium"', while Hazel Key says it's all due to a 'wilfulness on the part of gardeners and horticulturalists'.[18] *The Pelargonium and Geranium Society*, meanwhile, has debated its own designation for decades.[19] But perhaps the issue is less one of scientific misinterpretation than an indifference to taxonomy. Since this book will encompass the contribution of the *Pelargonium* to the botanist's herbarium and the persistent use of the African 'geranium' as a vehicle of expression and emotion, there should be no confusion if I use both botanical and vernacular names.

one

Out of Africa

🌿🌺🌿

I n 2011 the *International Register and Checklist of Pelargonium Cultivars* included more than 16,000 varieties. The number is stagger-ing, especially if we consider how few species these hybrids derive from. The largest group by far consists of variations on the upright scarlet zonal geranium, beloved of song and terracotta pot. This group has as its distant ancestors *Pelargonium zonale*, whose leaves have distinctive horseshoe-shaped markings, and *P. inquinans* or the 'staining pelargonium', named for the dye produced by its sap. The geraniums that trail from the balconies of Swiss chalets and clamber up palm trees in California, meanwhile, all derive from an ivy-leaved species called *Pelargonium peltatum*. The food and cosmetics industries, meanwhile, rely on aromatic oils that are extracted from the scented leaves of hybrids descended from crosses between the 'rose-geranium', *P. capitatum*, and either *P. graveolens* (whose name means 'strongly scented') or *P. radens* (named for its rasp-like leaves).[1] These are the species and cultivars that this book will mainly consider. But first, a bit of context.

In Africa

Pelargonium comprises a hugely diverse genus, consisting of around 280 species of evergreen and deciduous shrubs and sub-shrubs, climbers and scramblers, stem succulents, tuberous perennials and annual herbs. In the wild, plants range in height from a few centimetres

A postcard of palms and geraniums, California.

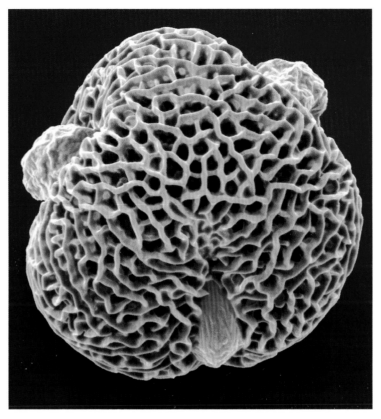

Coloured scanning electron micrograph (SEM) of a grain of pelargonium pollen.

to several metres. Their leaves come in all sorts of shapes and forms, the extent of which is evident if we consider the plants they were thought to resemble (and hence initially named after). These include hollyhock, carrot, sorrel, lady's mantle, parsley, birch, maple, oak, vine, ivy and samphire.[2] Pelargonium flowers, which are held as umbel-like clusters at the end of an erect stem, also come in various formations – resembling stars, saucers, funnels and claws – each of which suits the particular short- or long-tongued fly, bee, butterfly or bird which acts as its pollinator.[3]

What's even more astonishing is that all this variation occurs within a relatively small area. Thirty-two species of *Pelargonium* are dispersed quite widely: eighteen in East Africa; eight in Australasia;

two in Madagascar; two in Turkey; and one each on the islands of Tristan da Cunha and St Helena. All the others originate in the tip of southern Africa; and in particular, in the Cape Floristic Region (CFR), the smallest and most diverse of the six Floral Kingdoms. Ninety thousand square kilometres of land at the tip of the continent contains around 10,000 species; or, to put it another way, 0.5 per cent of Africa's landmass contains nearly 20 per cent of its flora.[4] The region is notable not only for the diversity of plants which grow there but because so many (70 per cent) are endemic. A relatively stable climate – there was no ice age at the Cape – is probably one reason why so many different kinds of plants exist today.[5]

For visitors, the effect can be overwhelming. In 1882, the British botanical artist Marianne North explored the area around Port Elizabeth and was amazed to see the ancestor of the familiar ivy-leaved geranium (*P. peltatum*) 'all tangled together' with gourds, plumbago, creepers and vines; when she came to paint her 'old friend', however, she gave it an orchid and a protea, two rather flashier Cape species, for company.[6] North's *An Old Friend and Its Associates in South Africa* is not so much a botanical study as a celebration of Darwin's vision of the 'grandeur' of life expressed in 'an entangled bank, clothed with many plants of many kinds'.[7] Where better to experience that grandeur than among the flora of the Cape?

Unlike other floral hotspots, such as the Amazon Rainforest, the Cape's diversity is mainly due to a few large clades (large groups of species with a common ancestor) which originated and steadily radiated, or adapted to life in different environments, within the region. The formation of new species typically requires the establishment of barriers to prevent populations from interbreeding. Natural selection can then take place as populations develop along different evolutionary paths, becoming increasingly different from each other. The Cape Floristic Region, itself 'virtually an island', encompasses numerous distinctive habitats, micro-climates (particularly in relation to patterns of rainfall), specialized pollinators, and a 'mosaic of different soil types'.[8] For example, the presence of isolated outcrops

Marianne North, *An Old Friend and its Associates in South Africa*, c. 1882, oil on board.

of sandstone within a sea of shale 'is likely to have encouraged the evolution of different species on each of the sandstone islands.'[9] Pelargoniums have found ecological niches everywhere from the sandy foreshore and mountain rock faces to desert and savannah, but around 150 species grow in the fynbos or nutrient-poor, fire-prone heathland which makes up around half of the CFR and which is 'characterised by exceptionally high numbers of highly localised species – those that are restricted to a single, small area, sometimes less than one square kilometre'.[10]

Today one in four South African plants are of 'conservation concern' due to climate change and agricultural and urban development, with 22 species of *Pelargonium* species identified as at high, very high or extremely high risk of extinction.[11] Conservation efforts have also been directed to pelargoniums in Australia, St Helena and Yemen – only discovered in 1999, the Yemenese *P. insularis* is already classified as 'critically endangered'.[12]

From the nineteenth century onwards, a growing awareness of the great diversity of *Pelargonium* resulted in its division into subgroups or sections. The most substantial revision of the genus, however, has taken place in the last 40 years, beginning with the work of a team of botanists at the University of Stellenbosch, led by J.J.A. van der Walt, which resulted in the three-volume *Pelargoniums of Southern Africa* (1977–88). Ellaphie Ward-Hilhorst contributed over 300 illustrations and *Pelargonium ellaphieae*, itself now endangered, was named in her honour. More recently, the advent of DNA sequencing has opened up the whole matter once again as scientists begin to explore the phylogenetic, or long-term evolutionary, kinships between groups of species. New assessments have been made of the rate and causes of diversification – from the 'nested radiations of closely related species' within the Cape winter-rainfall region, which seem to have begun eighteen million years ago,[13] to the relationships between South African and Australasian species,[14] and even between the different genera in the Geraniaceae family. Research suggests that 'the evolution of the Geraniaceae is marked by the dispersal of ancestors from Southern

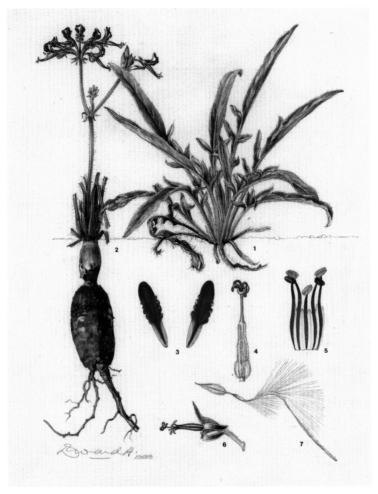

Ellaphie Ward-Hilhorst, *Pelargonium ellaphieae*, watercolour.

Africa to cold, temperate and often disturbed habitats in the rest of world.'[15]

Pelargonium has now been reclassified into two subgenera, in each of which a correlation can be seen between chromosome size and geographical distribution. The first is 'Pelargonium', whose small-chromosomed members account for around 80 per cent of all species. These plants are found in the winter-rainfall region of the Cape (the area that has a Mediterranean-style climate of warm, dry summers

P. magenteum in the arid Tanqua Basin, South Africa.

P. cortusifolium near Lüderitz on the coast of Namibia, 2003.

and cool, wet winters), and include 'the parents of most scented leaved varieties, the Angel pelargoniums and the Uniques, as well as the species, *P. cucullatum*, from which all Regal pelargoniums have been developed'.[16] The members of the other sub-genus, 'Ciconium', have large-sized chromosomes and include the ancestors of zonal and ivy-leaved pelargoniums.

Always Something New

The collection of South African plants, and their dispersal around the world, began at the end of the sixteenth century – a hundred years after the Portuguese navigator Bartolomeu Dias rounded the Cape of Good Hope in search of a route to India. The great era of botanical exploration had just started, and the spice ships of the Dutch East India Company (VOC) were perfectly placed to carry plants – valuable both as potentially useful commodities and as symbols of colonial possession – back to Europe. Since living specimens were difficult to transport successfully at this time, the cargo largely consisted of seeds, bulbs and dried plants, which were difficult enough to keep dry and free from damage by rodents. Merchant ships stopped off at many ports and early record-keeping was haphazard, so it was often unclear where exactly particular specimens had been collected. The first Cape plant listed in the botanical garden of the University of Leiden in 1597, a tough protea, was thought to be thistle from Madagascar.[17]

The first description of a pelargonium growing in Europe occurs in a text of 1633; and, as the plant was considered a native of India, it was

P. triste near Worcester in the Breede River Valley, South Africa.

P. triste at Woottens Nursery, Wenhanston, Suffolk. 2010.

designated, in lengthy, pre-Linnaean nomenclature, 'Sweet Indian Storks bill, or painted Storks bill: and in Latine, *Geranium Indicum odoratum flore maculato*'. In fact, the plant originated in the sandy flats and slopes near the Table Bay settlement. The London apothecary Thomas Johnson included the stork's bill, which had 'not as yet beene written about by any that I know', in his revised edition of Gerard's *The Herball or General Historie of Plants*. The *Herball* claimed to list all plants growing in Britain and Johnson noted that *Geranium Indicum* had 'as of late been brought into this kingdom by the industry of Mr John Tradescant.' Johnson had visited Tradescant's house in Lambeth and had seen the plant 'in flower about the end of July, 1632, being the first time that it flowered with the owner thereof'.[18] Previously gardener to Charles I, John Tradescant (the elder) was famous as a collector; his house contained a museum, the Ark, that eventually formed the basis of Oxford's Ashmolean Museum. Tradescant sought out novelties wherever he

'Geranium triste',
Plate 110 in Jacques-
Phillipe Cornut,
Canadensium plantarum
(Paris, 1635).

could find them – 'any thing that is strang [sic]' appealed.[19] In this case, his source was the Parisian nurseryman, René Morin, whose catalogue had included the Indian Stork's Bill since 1621.[20] Johnson does not say anything more about the plant, perhaps because it was more 'strang' than impressive. The leaves, which have been compared variously to a fern, a carrot and a tansy, are fine and divided, and the flowers small and pale yellow with a brownish-purple centre. These have a sweet clove-like scent but, as another apothecary, John Parkinson, pointed out, 'in the night onely, and not at all in the day time, as refusing the Sunnes influence, but delighteth in the Moones appearance'.[21] In 1635, the French physician Jacques-Phillipe Cornut, another client of Morin's, described and illustrated the plant under the name 'geranium triste' (*tristis* being Latin for sad).[22]

The pelargonium's most distinctive feature was its fat tuber, beetroot-red inside, which might initially have been thought to provide food for the long sea voyage.[23] Parkinson and Johnson would have been on the look-out for therapeutic uses for what they assumed to be a new variety of *Geranium*, a genus that had been used in European medicines for hundreds of years. Culpeper's *Herbal* of 1653, for example, advocated various species in the treatment of everything from colic to kidney stones, internal bleeding and a 'hot brain'.[24] Parkinson concluded that while 'both rootes and leaves' of the new introduction might be 'lettice for Indians lippes', he himself thought it 'tasteth somewhat sower'.[25]

The herbalists were unaware of the extensive therapeutic uses of pelargoniums by southern African tribespeople. Tubers of the sad geranium (*P. triste*) as well as those of *P. cucullatum*, *P. luridum*, *P. rapaceum* and *P. reniforme* were commonly roasted, infused or decocted to create astringent antidiarrhetics. The sap of the leaves of *P. peltatum* was considered an antiseptic for sore throats, and bathing in a decoction of

P. cucullatum on Signal Hill above Cape Town with Table Mountain in the background.

the root of *P. alchemilloides* was thought to reduce fever. The stems and leaves of *P. inquinans* were pounded to produce both a deodorant and a remedy for headaches and colds, while those of *P. betulinum* were steamed to create a camphor-like soothing vapour for coughs and other chest problems. The powdered root of *P. luridum*, when mixed with hippo or python fat and smeared all over, was thought to render a man sexually irresistible. Should pregnancy result, *P. grossularioides* induced abortion.[26] And so on.

Although some early collectors experimented with the pharmacological uses of pelargoniums (Paul Hermann, of whom more below, used *P. cucullatum* in an enema 'against the Cholick, Stone and difficulty of Urine, with good success') their novelty inspired greater interest than their utility.[27] By the end of the seventeenth century, as botanical exploration and trade gathered momentum, the old medical school physic gardens had largely become 'repositories for samplings of the flora of Europe's colonies'.[28]

The exploration of the Cape began properly, if slowly, after 1652, when the VOC established a permanent settlement and a Company Garden at Table Bay. Stopping there on his way to Sri Lanka in 1672, the company's Medical Officer, Paul Hermann, investigated the sandy outcrops of Table Mountain and among his finds was a two-metre tall shrub with pink flowers and large upward-facing leaves, which was later named *P. cucullatum*, or the hooded-leaf pelargonium. Hermann could hardly have imagined that this vigorous, rather ungainly shrub would become the ancestor of a group of exquisitely showy cultivars known as Regals or Martha Washingtons. His interest was in collecting and by the time he returned to Leiden to become Professor of Botany, Hermann had discovered eight further species of this newly fascinating genus.[29] In the decades that followed, more and more plants were sent back by the VOC, especially after the development of greenhouses provided a way of keeping the plants alive.[30] One of the first tasks undertaken by the Hortus Medicus in Amsterdam, founded in 1682 by Joan Huydecoper and Jan Commelin, was the construction of a glasshouse and among its first residents were two other important

P. zonale. Watercolour by Jan Moninckx in *Hortus Botanicus Amsterdans*
(Amsterdam, 1690).

pelargoniums from the scrubby hills of the southern Cape.[31] The first
was the zonate pelargonium (*P. zonale*), which Jan Moninckx illustrated
'stiffly' as if it were a little tree in *Hortus Botanicus Amsterdans* (1690).[32]
The other, sent to Commelin in 1700, was the scrambling ivy-leaved
geranium, *P. peltatum*.[33] By the beginning of the eighteenth century, then,

P. zonale in the Swartberg Pass. *P. peltatum* in the Little Karoo
near Calitzdorp.

the ancestors of the main groups of modern geraniums – Zonal, Ivy-leaved and Regal – had arrived in Holland.[34]

The Dutch had led the way in the plant business since the tulip-mania of the 1630s, with Leiden and Amsterdam operating as clearing houses for the northern European circulation of plants, seeds and knowledge. The British interest in exotics, which had rather lagged behind, intensified after the 1689 accession of William of Orange and Mary led to the adoption of Dutch fashions and Dutch garden-ers. The most notable was William Bentinck, later Earl of Portland, who, as Superintendent of the Royal Gardens, installed three huge 'glass cases' at Hampton Court to house the ever-growing royal collec-tion of tender exotics.[35] More generally, the success of those plants in northern Europe depended upon, and showcased, the development of glasshouses and 'stoves' (heated houses) during the seventeenth and early eighteenth century. Their availability, and efficiency, 'inevi-tably governed the population of tender plants'.[36]

The Chelsea Physic Garden acquired a glasshouse in 1684 and pelargoniums were cultivated there from 1690, when Bentinck presented the Society of Apothecaries with specimens of *P. cucullatum* and *P. capitatum*; by 1706, *P. gibbosum*, called 'gouty' because of its swollen joints, was also reported to be flourishing in the dry (and heated) 'stove'. Slowly the collection grew. One of the conditions that Sir Hans Sloane had imposed when he leased his land to the Apothecaries was that the Garden should supply the Royal Society annually with 50 specimens of dried and preserved plants; in 1724, the entire batch came from the Geraniaceae family, including six pelargoniums.[37]

The biggest collectors of 'Cape Cranesbills' at this time were wealthy individuals, many of whom commissioned catalogues in which to memorialize their treasures. One was the apothecary James Sherard, who kept a large garden of rare plants at his estate in Eltham in Kent and who employed the German-born botanist Johann Jakob Dillenius (later the first professor of botany at Oxford) to produce a *Hortus Elthamensis* (1732). As I noted in the Introduction, Dillenius suggested that the seven 'African geraniums' included might go by the name 'pelargonium'. Less concerned about the nomenclature, but even more enthusiastic about the plants, was the Revd Henry Compton, Lord Bishop of London and a great supporter of William and Mary. Compton, who maintained a 36-acre garden at Fulham Palace, was the first in Britain to grow many imported species. He had a particular interest in plants from the American colonies, from where his missionaries were instructed to send seeds, but he also acquired 'a very large and rare collection of *Pelargonium*', the most important of which was *P. inquinans*, the other species ancestor of the garden zonal.[38]

The plants kept circulating, albeit in narrow circles. Compton sent specimens to his sister-in-law, Mary Compton, Countess of Dorset, who passed them on to Mary Capel Somerset, the Duchess of Beaufort and one of the great patrons of eighteenth-century natural history in all its forms.[39] Beginning in the 1690s, the Duchess of Beaufort gradually accumulated one of the largest collections of exotic plants in England. (A 1699 catalogue listed 750 species.) She solicited seeds from the curators of botanical and physic gardens all over Europe, and hired George London, Bentinck's deputy at Hampton Court and founder of the Brompton Park Nursery, to supply her with plants, seeds and dried specimens.[40] Her head gardeners, William Oram (at Beaufort House in Chelsea) and John Adams (Badminton in Gloucestershire), were also instructed to track down unusual specimens. 'There is not a Garden within ten miles of London,' wrote Oram to Adams, 'wherther ther is Colexsions of plants but I have ben in.'[41] The Duchess assiduously noted the sources of these, prepared a twelve-folio herbarium of dried specimens (now in the Natural History Museum in London) and corresponded regularly on botanical matters with her friend and Chelsea neighbour, Sir Hans Sloane. 'When I get into storys of plants,' she wrote to him, 'I know not how to get out.'[42]

The success of the Badminton collection relied on the magnificent greenhouses and a 100-foot stove that the Duchess had built 'to rival the queen's'.[43] William Sherard, John Sherard's brother and a former pupil of Hermann's, served briefly as Supervisor of Greenhouses and boasted that Badminton would soon 'out-do any yet in Europe being furnished with all conveniences imaginable, and a good stock of plants, to which I have added above fifteen hundred, and shall daily procure more from my correspondents abroad'.[44] The *Hortus Kewensis* credits the Duchess of Beaufort with the introduction into English gardens of the zonal and ivy-leaved pelargonium. Some of her plants came from Sloane, and she returned the favour; it's likely that many of the pelargoniums presented by Chelsea Physic Garden to the Royal Society in 1724 originated in her collection.[45] The Duchess was much admired for a 'Nursing Care scarce any Plant (tho' from the most distant Climates) can withstand'.[46] Oram and Adams, who presumably did most of the nursing for her, don't often get a mention.

There seemed no end to the excitement of new introductions. 'I doe believe I may modestly affirme', wrote John Aubrey, that there is now, 1691, ten times as much gardening about London as there was Anno 1660; and wee have been, since that time, much improved in forreign plants, especially since about 1683, there have been exotick plants brought into England no lesse than seven thousand.[47]

But that was only the start. Year on year, the botanist James Petiver presented the Royal Society with a ever longer 'Account of diverse Rare plants, lately observed in several Curious Gardens about London'. In 1711, he thanked

that curious botanist, Dr Hermann, for the discovery of all these beautiful Cranesbills, which of later years have been the greatest ornaments in our finest gardens, viz at Hampton Court, Kensington, Fulham, Oxford, Chelsea, Hoxton, Enfield, Mitcham, &c.[48]

It wouldn't be long before less fine, and further-flung, gardens were able to share in the bounty, but first the bounty itself was to multiply beyond anyone's expectations.

In the 150 years since the 'sad geranium' had first created a stir, the introduction of new species remained at a steady trickle. Towards the end of the eighteenth century, however, the pace picked up. Plant-hunters increasingly ventured into the interior of the Cape, an area that Sir Joseph Banks, who had briefly stopped there on the way to Australia with Captain Cook, had identified as an 'untapped resource'.[49] Determined to establish the reputation of the Royal Garden at Kew as a rival to those at Paris and Vienna, Banks persuaded George III to appoint a designated plant-hunter to seek out new and unusual specimens. In 1772, the first man to hold the post, Francis Masson, sailed with Cook's second expedition as far as Cape Town where he spent the next three years. Masson made three expeditions 'into the country', accompanied on two occasions by Carl Thunberg, a pupil of Linnaeus.[50] Masson described a landscape 'of exquisite beauty and fragrance' that was 'enamelled with the greatest number of flowers' he had ever seen.[51] He sent home seeds and 'a profusion of Plants', to the great delight of Banks, who noted that 'by means of these, Kew Garden has in great measure attained to that acknowleg'd superiority which it now holds over every similar Establishment in Europe'.[52] Thunberg named one of the genera they discovered *Massonia* and Masson, rather shyly, sent a specimen to Linnaeus, asking if that would be all right.

Although Masson's trip was an acknowledged success, he was aware that 'many rare plants' remained 'entirely unknown to us'.[53] In 1776 Masson returned to Cape Town and remained there for nine years. This trip was more complicated than the first, as relations between Britain and Holland gradually deteriorated. Another plant-hunter, William Paterson – sponsored by the Countess of Strathmore – had been accused by the Dutch of spying, and Masson was therefore instructed by the colony's Governor 'not to travel anywhere that took him within three hours of the coast'.[54] (A waylaid letter from Banks, instructing Masson to concentrate his efforts on the botanically uninteresting False Bay, may have been a hint that he too should do some spying.[55]) During the Anglo-Dutch War of 1780–84, Masson found himself isolated, with very few ships available to take home a collection of plants that, despite all the restrictions, was 'very considerable and curious'.[56] Eventually many of Masson's specimens did make their way back to Kew, where a new greenhouse had to be built to house them.[57] The second edition of *Hortus Kewensis* (1810–13) features almost 1,000 Masson introductions, including 183 species of *Erica* (heaths) and 102 of *Pelargonium*.[58] Both would become staples of the Victorian garden.

After the British took control of the Cape, the balance of power in the pelargonium-hunting world shifted. But although expeditions to the region (known as Cape Colony until 1910) continued, Banks and others turned their attention to North American and Australasian plants. Among the plants collected, and illustrated, on the 1768–71 *Endeavour* voyage were *P. australe* and *P. inodurum*, found in Tolaga Bay,

P. inodurum from New Zealand. Watercolour on paper by Frederick Polydore Nodder, from a sketch made on the *Endeavour* voyage by Sydney Parkinson.

on the North Island of New Zealand. But plants did not only travel from the colonies to London; the city was a hub in an increasingly global market of seeds and knowledge. Colonial exporters were also importers. Before the War of Independence, a prime source of North American plants was the Philadelphia garden of the 'King's Botanist', John Bartram, a garden which eventually contained more than 200 native species. But when in 1760, Bartram decided to build a green-house to house 'plants for winter's diversion', his London partner-in-trade Peter Collinson knew exactly what was needed to 'furnish it'. Both Quakers, Collinson and Bartram nevertheless shared a love of 'fine, showey specious plants'.[59] 'I will send thee seeds of Gerani-ums', Collinson wrote. 'They have a charming variety and make a pretty show in a green-house; but contrive and make a stove in it, to give heat in severe weather.'[60]

Before and after Independence, Americans were keen to keep up with European fashion and by the end of the century the geranium's pretty show became increasingly available. Two species in particular seem to have become popular. The 'scarlet geranium' (*P. inquinans*) was mentioned by both Thomas Jefferson, who displayed it at Monticello and in the White House, and William Faris, a middle-class clockmaker from Annapolis who overwintered his plants in his cellar.[61] Also popu-lar was the 'rose geranium' (*P. capitatum*), which was listed among the houseplants held at the Virginia estate of Lady Jean Skipwith in the 1780s and which, in 1803, launched the career of horticultural entre-preneur Grant Thorburn.[62] Thorburn was selling painted terracotta pots in a New York street market when he came across a man selling 'rose-geraniums'. 'This was the first time that I ever heard that there was a geranium in the world', he later recalled, but as soon as he intro-duced plant to decorative pot, Thorburn was well on his way to a 'blooming fortune'.[63] By 1821, William Cobbett was issuing 'the American gardener' with instructions on how to grow a geranium from seed and cuttings, declaring that it 'wants *hardiness only* to make it the finest flower-plant of which I have any knowledge.'[64] Cobbett gardened in frost-prone Long Island. The Mediterranean climate of

Geraniums line the beach in Orange County, California.

California was to prove much more amenable to the African imports. Today ten pelargonium species and two hybrids have naturalized along the state's southern coast and in the winter of 2003, conservationists removed 765 'feral' zonals from Santa Cruz Island.[65] The geranium was well and truly out of Africa.

two

New Familiars

❦

The introduction of pelargoniums was part of a full-blown revolution in European botany. By the end of the eighteenth century, colonial plant-collecting had tripled the number of known plants and it would have been impossible to keep track or make sense of all the new species had botanists not decided to adopt a single and accessible way of organizing them.[1] Linnaeus's *Species Plantarum* (1753) was the right book at the right time. It proposed two things – the replacement of lengthy descriptive names with a Latin binomial (genus followed by species) and the soon-to-be-discredited sexual system, in which plants were classified according to the number of their stamens and pistils. The virtue of the system, argues Lisbet Koerner, 'consisted neither in its faithfulness to the natural order (it was patently artificial), nor in its inherent logic. But its workaday logic appealed to both learned men and novices.'[2] It also appealed to women and botany came to be regarded as an activity for which they were particularly suited. Eighteenth-century women 'collected plants, drew them, studied them, and named them, taught their children about plants, and wrote popularizing books on botany'.[3]

In this chapter, I will consider the geranium's place in those various endeavours: its representation in paint, print and paper collage; the first attempts to make it a metaphor; and the sociable, sometimes intimate, regard with which its owners came to view the horticultural newcomer.

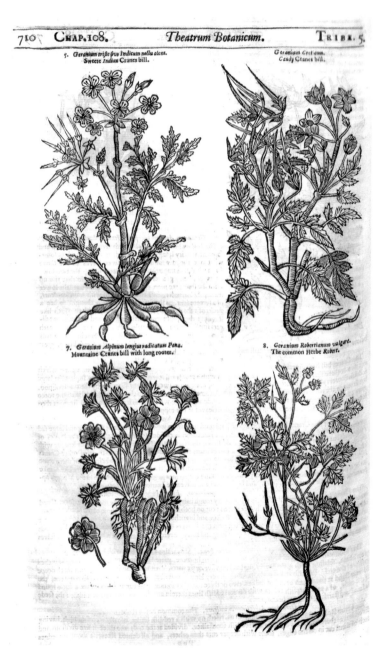

5. *Geranium triste sive Indicum noctu olens.*
Sweete *Indian* Cranes bill.

Geranium Creticum.
Candy Cranes bill.

7. *Geranium Alpinum longius radicatum Pona.*
Mountaine Cranes bill with long rootes.

8. *Geranium Robertianum vulgare.*
The common Herbe *Robert.*

Plate from John Parkinson, *Theatrum Botanicum* (London, 1640). The pelargonium
is top left.

'Geranium Noctuolens Aethiopicum', engraving from Jacob Breyne, *Exoticarum Plantarum Centuria Prima* (1678).

Picturing Pelargoniums

There are various reasons why one might want to illustrate a pelargonium and each results in a different kind of image. What is valuable
for one viewer is irrelevant to another. The first European repre-
sentations were by and for apothecaries interested in the possible
medical properties of plants and they therefore emphasize their
potentially useful roots and stems rather than their flowers. A typical

Pierre-Joseph Redouté, *P. tetragonum,* Plate 23 of Charles-Louis L'Héritier, *Geraniologia*
(1787–8).

P. tetragonum. Digital specimen image from the Herbarium Berolinense.

example is the 'Indian crane's bill' (*P. triste*) in John Parkinson's *Theatrum Botanicum* (1640), one of the last traditional herbals. Although the plant was recognized as 'new, rare and strange', it is neverthless crammed onto the corner of page featuring a group of its European cousins of supposedly similar 'qualities and uses'. The simplified woodcuts give just enough detail to distinguish each from its neighbours. The crisply delineated engravings of Jacob Breyne's *Exoticarum Plantarum Centuria Prima* (1678) couldn't be more different. Here *P. triste* features as a representative of 'the first century of exotic plants', each of which is given a page-sized portrait designed to highlight its wow factor. The pelagonium's dramatic focus is its huge dark tuber.

The advent of copper engraving meant that artists were able to record minute differences between species, allowing them to be more accurately identified and classified by botanists.[4] Once the Linnaean sexual system was adopted, prominence was placed on the structure of the flower (filling up space previously occupied by a lengthy descriptive text). We can see this emphasis in the work of Pierre-Joseph Redouté, best known today for his paintings of the Empress Josephine's roses. Redouté had been trained 'in the techniques of dissection and the details of plant anatomy' by L'Héritier and was the main illustrator of his *Geraniologia*.[5] His drawings combine an elegantly idealized portrait of stem and flower and, below, a little narrative of the plant's reproductive cycle from flowering to seed dispersal. Redouté also makes sure that the pelargonium's distinctive seven stamens are clearly visible; something that was difficult to achieve with a flattened herbarium specimen.

Other decisions concerned scale and colour. If the plant was too large for the plate, its size might be indicated by the inclusion of a single life-size detail or by presenting it in two parts, with the lower stem and roots alongside the upper stem and flower. Colour was originally applied by hand. The first botanical book whose plates were printed in colour was John Martyn's *Historia Plantarum Rariorum* (1728–37). But a vivid pinkish-red is not all that distinguishes the *P. papilionaceum* (or the butterfly stork's bill), engraved and coloured by Elisha Kirkall after the drawing by Jacob van Huysum. Van Huysum's emphasis on the plant's habit of growth is also unusual: we might compare the same plant in Dillenius's *Hortus Elthamensis*.[6] Although Martyn's book was intended for fellow members of the Botanical Society (whose seal is prominently displayed on the image), this simplified and stylized image has 'more in common with the virtuosity of Oriental brushwork than with the more scientific products of European plant illustration'.[7]

'Geranium africanum arborescens, malvae folio', from Dillenius, *Hortus Elthamensis* (London, 1732).

'Geranium africanum arborescens, malvae folio', intaglio engraving by Elisha Kirkhall after the drawing by Jacob van Huysum, in John Martyn, *Historia Plantarum Rariorum*.

'Geranium Indicum
Nocte Odoratum',
from Abraham
Munting, *Phytographia
Curiosa* (Utrecht,
1702).

GERANIUM INDICUM NOCTE ODORATUM.

There was often overlap between the informative intention of
the botanical treatise and the decorative ambition of the florilegium
(literally, a gathering of flowers). At his publishers' request, Abraham
Munting presented the plant portraits in his botanical work within,
or floating above, a classical landscape. A specimen of 'night scented
Indian geranium' (*P. triste*) is depicted on the promontory of a grassy
hillock with a temple in the background; the plant is so large and im-
posing (like a giant tree) that its tuberous root hangs over the edge.
(In my copy of the 1702 engraving, the flowers have been miscoloured
red, but in truth that's the least of its problems.) A better balance of
botanical and pictorial interest can be found in Everard Kickius's
watercolours of the Duchess of Beaufort's collection (the paintings

P. paltatum. Watercolour by Everard Kickius, from the Duchess of Beaufort's Codex, 1703–5.

'December'. Engraving by Henry Fletcher after the painting by Pieter Casteels, from Robert Furber, *The Twelve Months of Flowers* (1730).

themselves complemented her twelve-volume herbarium).[8] Kickius's portrait of the ivy-leaved geranium (*P. peltatum*) is drawn to scale and uprooted, in the botanical style, but is given a decorative setting, in the florilegia tradition.

Although books like the Beaufort Codex were intended for private consumption – a 'permanent portable substitute for the impermanent and fixed, a garden and its plants'[9] – a commercial

market for luxury flower books was also emerging.[10] In 1730 the
Duchess of Beaufort was one of a select group of aristocratic sub-
scribers to what is thought to be the first illustrated nursery catalogue.
The Twelve Months of Flowers was produced by Robert Furber, 'Gardiner,
at Kensington', to showcase a stock of 400 different species and
varieties. Each hand-coloured print depicts a sumptuous bouquet
(from a painting by the Flemish artist Pieter Casteels) keyed to a list
of plants that would flower that month.[11] For clear identification, and
in the Flemish tradition, 'every flower faces front, arranged separately
and distinctly from its companions'; the 'details and dissections essential to botany are superfluous' here.[12] The December selection includes
an early mention of a variegated or 'strip'd-leav'd geranium', at number 21, and, at number 17, in central position, a 'scarlet geranium'.[13]

Of all the wealthy patrons of this period, none compares with
Lady Margaret Cavendish Bentinck, wife of the second Duke of Port-
land. Her Buckinghamshire home of Bulstrode was known as the
Hive for its extensive collections of natural history, decorative and
fine arts; collections which, after her death, took 38 days to auction
off. Bulstrode also functioned as an 'incubator of Linnaean botany'.[14]
Guided by her 'botanical master' and curator, the Revd John Light-
foot, she entertained all the leading figures of the time, including
Sir Joseph Banks and Daniel Solander, just back from Australia, and
G. D. Ehret, the German illustrator of Linnaeus, who painted her
flowers and tutored her daughters. The Duchess's great friend Mary
Delany was also frequently present. Widowed for a second time in her
seventies, Delany began to spend her summers at Bulstrode, which
she felt to be a *noble school* for contemplations', and it was there, in
1772, that she invented a 'new way of imitating flowers', one that drew
on the styles of both floral painting and the *hortus siccus* (literally, dry
garden).[15] Noting a similarity in tone between a piece of red Chinese paper and the geranium flower on her table, Delany cut out
petal shapes and, using more coloured paper for the leaves and stalk,
created a representation of what was probably a cultivar of *P. fulgidum*
(named for its gleaming flowers). When the Duchess entered the

room, she reputedly mistook the paper petals for real ones and 'a new work was begun from that moment'.[16] By the time she lost her sight ten years later, Delany had created an impressive 'Flora Delanica' of nearly 1,000 life-sized 'paper mosiacks' set against a distinctive black background.

What Erasmus Darwin, another friend, described as Delany's 'mimic bowers' reveal considerable botanical knowledge as well as artistic skill. She carefully included the right number of stamens and pistils (according to the Linnaean sexual system) and annotated each drawing with its Latin binomial.[17] The largest group in the collection consists of plants she terms 'geranium' – most of which are pelargoniums. For the first few years, she worked her way through the Duchess's glasshouses and gardens. In May 1775, for example, she visited the kitchen garden stove and came again upon *P. fulgidum*,

Mary Delany,
P. fulgidum, 1755.
Collage of coloured
papers with
bodycolour and
watercolour.

the 'scarlet geranium' that she herself had brought from her father's collection, in full flower and 'high beauty'.[18] Eventually, though, Delany turned to the glasshouses of her friends and acquaintances. A quick survey of the provenance of her pelargoniums (noted carefully on the back of each collage) gives a sense of the social round of aristocratic plant-lovers in this period. Three (*P. peltatum, P. inquinans* and *P. alchemelloïdes*) came from the nearby estate of Sir George Howard; another (*P. gibbosum*) from Miss Jennings, her London pupil 'in the paper mosaic work'; *P. triste* was supplied by the Chelsea Physic Garden. None of these species were rarities by this time, but Delany's notes also reveal an acquaintance with 'newly introduced exotics within three or four years of the first date of introduction'.[19] In 1776, she was asked to show her work to George III, Queen Charlotte and Lord Bute, a powerful 'trio of enthusiastic botanists'.[20] Charlotte – who had studied painting with Kew's resident artist, Francis Bauer – presented Delany with a decorative set of tools, while George III instructed Joseph Banks to send her plants from Kew, including five of Masson's newly arrived pelargoniums.[21] Another two were supplied by Lee and Kennedy's nursery at Hammersmith. We don't know how much they charged her, but around this time, Telfords of York and Perfects of Pontefract were offering geraniums 'of sorts' for between one and two and a half shillings per plant – just sixpence less than a builder's daily wage.[22]

The Duchess of Portland also collected – and Delany represented – a considerable number of British species, particularly wild-flowers, and over the breadth of her collection, Delany's collages seem to create a 'dialogue between natives and exotics'.[23] Other artists liked to match a foreign rarity with its 'humble compeers' in the same drawing, with the combination of South African pelargonium and the European 'wild geranium' a particularly appealing one.[24] The Dutch artist Henriette Knip gathers them in a loose posy, adding a ranunculus for good measure.

The decorative value of plants was not confined to the canvas and the page. Many books combined the function of floral record

Henriette Knip. *Ranuculus, pelargonium and wild geranium.*

and pattern book. The 1732 reprint of Furber's book, *The Flower Garden Displayed*, was marketed as a 'very useful' source of floral motifs for 'Painters, Carvers, Japaners, etc, also for the Ladies, as Patterns for working, and Painting in Water-Colours; or Furniture for the Closet.'[25] Seat coverings, fire screens and clothes were also lavishly embellished with flowers. Some years before she turned to paper collages, Mary Delany made a black silk court dress onto which she embroidered a Rococo border of over 200 flowers, including a scarlet *P. inquinans.*[26]

Pelargonium radicatum.
Drawing by
Sydenham Edwards
engraved by Francis
Sansom for *Curtis's*
Botanical Magazine, no.
1718 (1 April 1815).

By the end of the century, the fashion for exotic plants was spreading ever wider. In 1787 William Curtis launched the first periodical
devoted to scientific horticulture, *The Botanical Magazine; or, Flower Garden Displayed* which, under the name *Curtis's Botanical Magazine*, is still
published today. Each issue contained three plant descriptions illustrated by a hand-coloured plate, 'always from the living plant'. These
became popular as templates for commercially produced textiles,
porcelain and other forms of domestic ornament, as were the plates
of John Edwards's *A Collection of Flowers* (1790). One of Edwards's
flowing compositions, combining what is probably a sprig of the

John Edwards, *A Collection of Flowers* (1790), folio 19.

rose-scented *P. graveolens* with the heart-shaped leaf of *P. cordifolium,* inspired William Pegg's design for the cover of a soup tureen made by the Derby Manufactuary in 1796.[27] And among the many floral wallpapers sold by the fashionable London decorator Joseph Trollope around this time, that featuring a geranium horseshoe leaf 'outstripped the rest in popularity'.[28]

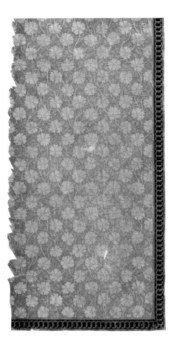

Block-printed wallpaper with geranium-leaf design, from the front room of 48 Manchester Street, Marylebone, *c.* 1790.

Derby soup tureen, cover and stand, porcelain, painted with botanical designs in enamel colours and gilt by William Pegg after drawings by John Edwards, *c.* 1796.

An Education in Geraniums

For late-eighteenth-century women, flowers were never merely decorative. Indeed the study of plants often found itself at the heart of debates about the value (and, for some, the dangers) of women's education. On the one hand, botany was presented as the perfect subject for mothers to teach their children.[29] It was considered easier than zoology, with the added advantage that, unlike animals, 'plants do not bleed'.[30] On the other hand, Linnaeus's proposal that plants be classified according to the number of their (male) stamens and (female) pistils gave a 'primacy to plant sexuality that no naturalist had before'.[31] 'Botanizing girls' were accused of exchanging 'the blush of modesty for the bronze of impudence'.[32]

Lessons often took the form of letters from one woman to another, or a conversation between a mother and her inquiring children.[33] One of the first, and most popular, of these books was Priscilla Wakefield's *An Introduction to Botany, in a Series of Familiar Letters*, which introduces Linnaean botany through a correspondence between two sisters; it ran to eleven editions between 1796 and 1811. While Wakefield consigns pelargoniums, 'of which our greenhouse displays such an amazing variety', to a footnote and her readers' 'own examination', *Botanical dialogues, between Hortensia and her four children, Charles, Harriet, Juliette and Henry*, published anonymously by Maria Elizabeth Jackson in 1797, directly addresses L'Héritier's 'new arrangement of the geranium family' into three distinct genera.[34] Hortensia instructs Juliette to look carefully at the flower in her hand, and 'you will see that the sub-divisions of the genera depend on the number of anther-bearing stamens'. Juliette counts seven and agrees with her mother that she's looking at a pelargonium, although she says she is 'sorry' that she can 'no longer call this plant the horse-shoe geranium'. Hortensia has no patience with such sentimentality – 'the zoned pelargonium will soon become equally familiar to you,' she snaps, and moves briskly on to Charles and his artichoke.[35]

Tutorials were also conducted through a guided tour of a poetic herbarium or botanical garden, in the manner of Erasmus Darwin's hugely popular *The Loves of the Plants* (1789), a poem with botanical footnotes, in which 83 species are imagined as everything from 'virtuous brides and tender mothers to attentive sisters, nymphs and shepherdesses' to 'laughing belles and wily charmers' to 'queens and amazons'.[36] Linnaeus had presented plant reproduction in conventional social terms; he spoke 'husbands' and 'wives' and described a flower's petals as a 'marriage bed', establishing a metaphor that Darwin and his followers adopted with glee. Suddenly plant-life was 'all about the all-pervading drive to find a mate and to reproduce', and the imaginations of poets ranged far beyond stamen and pistil.[37]

Darwin's combination of pastoral romance and scientific footnote was also widely imitated. Frances Arabella Rowden's *A Poetical Introduction to the Study of Botany* (1800), for example, includes this entry for the night-scented '*Geranium triste*':

> Now modest Cynthia leads her silv'ry car,
> And slowly rising shines the ev'ning star.
> The feather'd songsters sink to soft repose,
> And the gay flow'rs their nodding petals close.
> Now the meek vot'ry of these hours serene
> Sheds her mild odors o'er the shadowy scene;
> At her command *seven* gay Sylphs arise,
> And waft her fragrant incense to the skies;
> Through the wide air, link'd hand in hand, they sail,
> And scent with balmy sweets each passing gale.
> The love-lorn maiden now delights to stray,
> And pour her sorrows to the moon's pale ray;
> The faithful swain attunes his melting lyre,
> And strikes its notes as joy or pain inspire.
> Deep in his lonely cell the hoary sage
> With studious eye explores the letter'd page.
> The Poet's soul, with countless beauties fraught,

Soars through the realms of fancy and of thought:
His airy visions glow with heav'nly light,
And genius triumphs 'mid the shades of night.[38]

Rowden tries to stay true to her specimen's botanical characteristics (which a footnote elaborates further) while presenting its scent as inspiring 'the Poet's soul' in conventional classical surroundings. But the story doesn't stop there. The geranium might be a 'meek' votary of Cynthia, virgin goddess of the moon, but she is not above advertising herself as sexually available through the eager endeavours of the odour-wafting '*seven* gay Sylphs' – a direct allusion to the pelargonium's seven fertile stamens. The 'genius' that 'triumphs' is presumably that of the swain's poem, the legitimate fruit of 'male procreativity'.[39]

Other geraniums were even more risqué, largely by virtue of what William Cowper, in his poem *The Task* (1785), called the 'crimson honours' of the most popular varieties, and perhaps also because of the (seemingly) suggestive way in which their petals overlapped.[40] Sexy women, said Robert Rabelais (pseud.) in 1814, have 'pouting and geranium'd lips'.[41] It was an image (and a phrase) that would endure – for example, the kings of Tyrus wait in line for a 'geranium kiss' from Bob Dylan's Sad-Eyed Lady of the Lowlands.[42] Today some of us fake it with 'geranium' lipstick.

'The Geranium' (1795), by Thomas Erskine, was unusual in thinking about the form of the whole plant, rather than simply the flower's petals, and thus in figuring it as male. Erskine begins by describing the geranium's 'pale declining head' and the straight stalk which 'tempts our violating hands'. 'Sweet Sue' certainly can't resist and, after one gentle caress from her dewy palms, the plant is 'ripe to blow / The stems shall rise, the head shall glow'. A footnote earnestly assures readers that 'this description is Botanically true', but the poem quickly abandons any pretence to science to focus on Sue's 'strange raptures'.

Ah me cried Susan whence is this,
What strange tumultuous throbs of bliss,
Sure never mortal till this hour,
Felt such emotion at a flower[43]

The personification of the geranium was not, however, confined to the 'bliss botanic'.[44] Scientists like Erasmus Darwin, seeking to establish a continuity between all living organisms, flora and fauna, attributed to both sensation, movement and even, it seemed, something like mental alertness and social behaviour. If it was a little too much to claim 'absolute sense' for plants, argued the Philadelphia plantsman, John Bartram, 'yet they have such facilities as came so near it that we wanted a proper epithet or explanation.'[45] Bartram's son, William, also a botanist, pictured climbers in trees as 'leaning,

'Regal Geranium Cluster'.

extending, and like the fingers of the human hand, reaching to catch hold of what is nearest, just as if they had eyes to see with'.[46] A belief in the 'analogy of their organisation with ours', as Thomas Jefferson put it, opened up new ways of being familiar with geraniums.[47]

Friends in Adverse Fortune

Jefferson and his geraniums had a particularly sociable relationship. He first encountered the plants while ambassador to France in the 1780s and later enjoyed propagating specimens from cuttings, both at his Virginia home of Monticello and at the White House.[48] His friend Margaret Bayard Smith visited him at the White House in 1803 and was delighted to see that, in the window of his personal apartment, Jefferson had created 'stands for the flowers and plants which it was his delight to attend, and among his roses and geraniums was suspended the cage of his favourite mocking-bird, which he cherished with peculiar fondness.'

> How he loved this bird! How he loved his flowers! He could not live without something to love, and in the absence of his darling grandchildren, his birds and his flowers became objects of tender care.[49]

As Jefferson's Presidency came to an end, Smith wrote asking for a cutting of a particularly fine specimen 'which I understood you cultivated with your own hands':

> If you do not take it home with you, I entreat you to leave it with me. I cannot tell you how inexpressively precious it will be to my heart. It shall be attended with the assiduity of affection and watered with tears of regret each day I attend it, will I invoke the best blessings of Heaven on the most venerated of human beings!

Rembrandt Peale, *Rubens Peale with a Geranium*, 1801, oil on canvas.

How could he resist? Jefferson sent the plant to Mrs Smith, apologizing that it was 'in very bad condition, having been neglected latterly', but expressing his confidence that, under her 'nourishing hand', it would soon recover. 'If plants have sensibility,' he added, 'it cannot be but proudly sensible of her fostering attentions.'[50]

Another plant that seems sensible, and appreciative, of the attention paid to it is that portrayed in *Rubens Peale with a Geranium*. The son of the painter and naturalist Charles Willson Peale, Rubens was a keen botanist from a young age. A sickly child, he often endured the attentions of an unloved family physician and later recalled his delight on learning that the doctor had died. After throwing away the many potions and powders the doctor had prescribed, Rubens 'went into the garden and took the watering pot and watered my flowers which I was forbidden to do, after that time I gradually increased my strength and health.'[51]

In 1801, his brother Rembrandt (the family also included a Titian and a Raphaelle) painted Rubens with a favourite plant. Although the leaves, stalks and flowers of the geranium are clearly, almost anatomically, depicted, the painting's interest lies less in its botanical detail than in its presentation of a relationship of near visual equals – although the geranium (like Jefferson's, a scarlet *P. inquinans*) is rather taller than Rubens. Alexander Nemerov explores the parallel:

> The geranium rises out of its convex earthen pot just as Rubens's face rises from his convex white collar. The v-shape of the plant's rising stalks repeats the v of Rubens's lapels and white shirt front. The curve of two of the leftmost stalks echoes the locks of hair falling over Rubens's forehead. The triangular wisps of white collar at his jaw repeat the angle, thickness, and shape of the leaf immediately to his left. One edge of this leaf also picks up the line of his black collar. The central fold of this leaf, as well as its flared shape, repeats the shape of Rubens's nose, and the leaf as a whole repeats the size, shape, and orientation of Rubens's left hand, even down to the way the central fold repeats the gap between middle- and forefingers. Finally . . . the fingers of Rubens's *right* hand, resting partly within the pot, repeat the two pointed fronds [and, I'd add, the two beak-like seedpods] touching or nearly touching his hair.[52]

Perhaps Rubens had to interact with his geranium by touch because he was so short-sighted (he's peering over the top of one pair of glasses and holding another), but the painting certainly suggests that his affection was reciprocated. Rubens has his hand in the pot, presumably to check if the soil needs watering, and, as Nemerov points out, his fingers look as if they might almost take root.[53] But while man and plant are both well-dressed (in clothes and leaves respectively), they also share a rather droopy demeanour. The lowest of the plant's distinctive horseshoe leaves is brown at its edges and another has already fallen onto the table, a sign of weakness reinforcing the implication of the second pair of spectacles. In some ways, the painting is less interested in anthropomorphizing a plant than in showing how vegetative a man might be.

Peale was not the only one who believed that interacting with geraniums was 'healthful'. More generally, the study of plants was promoted (partly in response to claims of sexual impropriety) as 'affording a continual and engaging motive for air and exercise' and stimulating 'every curious mind'.[54] Plants had become therapeutic in a new way – not through the apothecaries' concoctions or infusions, but simply by being there. Floral interaction was thought to provide solace, especially for invalids (like the young Rubens Peale), widows (such as Mrs Delany), and presidents who missed their grandchildren. One did not even need to leave the house in order to experience what Rousseau, in *Reveries of the Solitary Walker* (1782), described as botany's 'recreation for the eyes, which in misfortune relaxes, amuses, and distracts the mind, and lifts the feeling of pain . . . Sweet scents, bright colours, and the most elegant of shapes seem to vie for the right to seize our attention.'[55] The poet and writer Charlotte Smith, who suffered from chronic rheumatism and depression, read Rousseau and agreed that botanizing could 'soothe' a 'wounded mind'.[56] She spoke rather fiercely of the study of plants as an antidote to the 'mawkish indolence', 'inanity' and 'torpid ignorance' that might render a woman 'burthensome to herself and uninteresting to others'.[57] And when bad weather prevented such a woman from getting out into the garden, she could turn her attention to the plants in her greenhouse. After all, as Cowper famously declared in *The Task*, 'who loves a garden, loves a green-house too':

Unconscious of a less propitious clime
There blossoms exotic beauty, warm and snug,
While the winds whistle and snows descend.[58]

Smith agreed. Her poem 'To a Geranium which flowered during the Winter' (1804) celebrates the way its 'cheerful hue' punctures the 'wintry gloom'. Flowers that could offer such relief were 'like friends in adverse fortune true'.[59]

Another woman who needs a geranium friend is Fanny Price, the heroine of Jane Austen's third novel, *Mansfield Park* (1814). Fanny is a poor girl living off the charity of her uncle and aunt. The family are anxious that she doesn't get ideas beyond her station and so limit her comforts. She is given as her bedroom a 'little white attic . . . close by the housemaids' but, after the daughters of the house finish their education, she also appropriates the schoolroom, or East room, as her own. Although it's badly furnished and unheated, for Fanny the room becomes a 'nest of comforts', a retreat to which she can retire in order to 'visit her plants' and to escape 'any thing unpleasant below'. One day after a particularly upsetting exchange (the cousins and their friends want her to take part in their improper theatricals), Fanny hurries upstairs, hoping that 'by giving air to her geraniums she might inhale a breeze of mental strength herself'.[60] Like Smith (and in the words of her favourite poet, Cowper), Fanny is looking for 'seclusion from a jarring world'.[61]

But it's more than a need for 'careful cultivation' that connects Fanny with the 'botanical transplant from warmer regions'.[62] The novel draws clear parallels between colonial and class uprooting. Fanny has been 'collected' by the Bertrams from her lower-middle-class home in Portsmouth, with the expectation that she will flourish (decoratively) in the enriched soil of Mansfield Park.

Charlotte Smith describes a similar process in 'To a Geranium'. The poem was included in her *Conversations introducing poetry: chiefly on subjects of natural history. For the use of children and young persons*, and thus begins, educationally, with a little background information.

> Native of Afric's arid lands,
> Thou, and thy many-tinctur'd bands,
> Unheeded and unvalued grew,
> While Caffres crush'd beneath the sands
> Thy pencil'd flowers of roseate hue.[63]

The young persons duly informed both of the plant's origins and its luck in escaping them, Smith goes on to describe the 'art' required to supply it with the appropriate 'tepid dew'. Finally, she concludes that the geranium (that is, pelargonium) that has been rescued from 'Afric's arid lands' is superior to native ('uncultur'd') geraniums which 'decline with the declining year':

> While in successive beauty new,
> Thine own light bouquets fresh appear,
> And marbled leaves of cheerful hue.

Here Smith employs the classic colonizers' rationale: that foreign raw material ('unheeded and unvalued' when not actually 'crush'd') is much improved by European culture (leaves become 'marbled', flowers 'pencill'd'). No wonder, then, that African plants 'naturalized in foreign earth' flower so profusely.

> As if in gratitude they blew,
> To hang, like blushing trophies forth,
> Thy pencill'd flowers of roseate hue.

The problem with Fanny Price (as far as the Bertrams are concerned) is that, for a while at least, she refuses to bloom in gratitude. Instead, she becomes a kind of colonizer herself – creating an 'establishment' in the East room (where she not only cultivates plants but reads books on China). The East room serves as a commentary on the larger landscapes of the novel: Sotherton estate where the novel's courtship plot takes place, and the plantations that Fanny's uncle Sir

Bertram had established in the West Indies. But for all its seeming disadvantages – it is small and cool (her aunt having 'stipulated for there never being a fire in it on Fanny's account') – the room functions as a glasshouse in which both Fanny and her geraniums can flourish and find culture. After all, an east-facing aspect means sun in the morning; a 'period of the day', noted garden-writer Jane Loudon,

Childe Hassam, *Summer Evening*, 1886, oil on canvas.

'when warmth is particularly agreeable'.[64] Like Smith's geraniums, Fanny acclimatizes successfully, so well in fact that she can no longer cope with the 'ceaseless tumult' of Portsmouth – her trip back is presented as the equivalent of a newly cultured geranium being forced to return to the trampling feet of the 'Caffres'. Mansfield, with its orderly parks and plants ('every thing opposite' to Portsmouth)

has become 'home'. For one thing, it isn't until she is reacquainted with 'confinement, bad air, bad smells' that Fanny realizes 'how much the beginnings and progress of vegetation had delighted her'.[65]

Fanny's own 'progress of vegetation' is mapped onto the progress of her moral, social and physical refinement. By the time that Sir Bertram returns from Antigua, installs a fire in the East room, and organizes Fanny's 'coming out' ball, she has grown 'worth looking at'. Not only is her complexion (her 'hue') now 'tinged with a blush', she 'must be grown two inches, at least, since October!' Sir Bertram, like a satisfied plant-hunter, concludes that Fanny's 'transplantation to Mansfield' has been a success.[66]

In many ways, as Barbara Hardy notes, 'Fanny Price anticipates the Victorian heroine.'[67] The figure of the solitary girl with her 'little Lamp and Book – / And one geranium –', as Emily Dickinson put it, was to become a staple of nineteenth-century literature and even persisted into twentieth-century film. But although the window-sill companion did not entirely lose its exotic appeal (Dickinson compared her geranium to a Turkish 'Sultana' and wrote that 'when the Humming birds come down – Geranium and I shut our eyes – and go far away'[68]), it mostly became a homely and thoroughly moral kind of friend. The good Victorian mother did not teach her children about the classification of plants and their methods of reproduction. Instead she harnessed geraniums as weapons in the fight against slovenliness, vanity and carelessness. There would be a new language of flowers to learn.

three

Bedding and Breeding

❧❦❧

B y 1816, it was already possible to be nostalgic about the days when 'the sight of an African geranium, in Yorkshire or Norfolk' had been an event. 'Now,' noted the botanist James Edward Smith, 'every garret and cottage window is filled with numerous species of that beautiful tribe'.[1] The next two chapters will explore the transformation of the geranium, in fact and in the popular imagination, from coveted hothouse exotic to 'filler' plant, the reliable mainstay of window boxes and bedding schemes. To a large extent, the way we think about geraniums today is a product of that makeover.

A variety of factors account for the proliferation of pelargoniums during the nineteenth century. One was the introduction of new technologies which would revolutionize horticulture – in particular, the new glass-and-iron greenhouse, which facilitated the hybridization and mass-production of plants, and the steam railway network, which distributed them. Industrialization also saw the rapid creation of an urban population whose rural ties were often (at least in legend) expressed through the desire to cultivate something, anything. Chapter Four will explore the re-invention of the geranium as a 'cottage exotic'.[2] Here, though, I'd like to begin by considering some pre-Victorian cousins, the exclusive pelargoniums of the Regency era. These were plants to be pictured with, as Queen Adelaide was in William Beechey's portrait of 1831.

Where once social status could be measured by possession of the most recently arrived African species, in the early nineteenth

'Le Géranium de Prusse', 1832, lithograph by Le Mercier, Paris: François et Louis Janet.

century, as consumption extended and became more conspicuous, the 'Fashionable World' competed for the latest showy cultivars from London's West End nurseries. Varieties with names like 'Waterloo', 'Royal George' and the 'Prince Regent's Geranium' occupied pride of place in the theatrical floral displays of Regency house parties.[3] During the London season, nurseries leased plants by the night, the week or the month, with orders ranging from a few pots to several hundred. All manner of elaborate containers, baskets and stands were placed in conservatories, specially constructed garden pavilions and even drawing rooms – 'floral borders were simulated indoors with moss beds interspersed with pots of flowering and exotic shrubs'.[4]

The new cultivars were the result of an explosion in hybridizing that took place both in the burgeoning nursery trade and in the homes

Queen Adelaide, painted by William Beechey and engraved by S. W. Reynolds, 1831.

of wealthy enthusiasts such as Lady Mary Hussey, Robert Banks Jenkinson – the second Earl of Liverpool, and Prime Minister from 1815 to 1822 – and, most notably, his cousin, Robert H. Jenkinson and Sir Richard Colt Hoare. Often the same cultivars appeared under different names – for example, what Lady Mary called 'P. husseyanum'

92.

'Pelargonium husseyanum'. Plate no. 92 in Robert Sweet, *Geraniaceae*. Engraving by
J. Watts after a drawing by Edwin Dalton Smith.

was also known as Brown's Duke of York Geranium, and, by Colt Hoare, as 'P. Robertsonii'.[5] By the 1820s, Colt Hoare was able to boast 600 varieties in his conservatory at Stourhead while an impressive 500 could be purchased from the most fashionable of nurseries, Colvill's of King's Road.[6] Among both professional and amateur English florists, William Cobbett observed in 1829, the pelargonium had become what 'the tulip and hyacinth are with the Dutch florists: they spare no expense in erecting propagation-houses and conservatories for it, they have shows of it, they give a high-sounding name to every new variety, and whole works have been published laudatory of its beauties.'[7]

Those 'whole works' – the two volumes of Henry Andrews's *Geraniums* (1805–6) and the five volumes of *Geraniaceae* (1820–30), by Robert Sweet, foreman at Colvill's – are the only record we now have of once prized cultivars. Of course Britain wasn't the only place in which pelargonium mania had taken hold and, in compiling his great synthetic work, Sweet drew on books published in Paris (L'Héritier, de Candolle, Cavanilles), Vienna (Nickolaus von Jacquin) and Berlin (Carl Ludwig Willdenow), as well as those we've already considered from Leiden (Hermann), Amsterdam (Burman, Commelin) and London (Dillenius, Martyn, Aiton, Andrews). Between 1825 and 1843, Leopold Trattinick, the Austrian court botanist, published *Neue Arten von Pelargonien deutschen Ursprunges*, a four-volume 'supplement' to Sweet, detailing 400 hybrids from Germany.

There were so many new plants (both species and cultivars) that further classification was needed. While Andrews simply organized his plants into 'the Elegant', 'the Magnificent' and 'the Handsome', Sweet argued for the introduction of ten new genera. Although such extreme action was quickly rejected – in 1824 the great Swiss taxonomist Augustin Pyrame de Candolle instead subdivided the genus *Pelargonium* into twelve sections – some of Sweet's suggested divisions, such as Jenkinsonia (eleven species) or Hoarea (80 species), have remained.[8]

Among the few first-generation hybrids that is still available (if not in every garden centre), *Pelargonium x* Ardens, the 'glowing geranium', is one of the finest.[9] Flowering in the northern hemisphere in the late winter and early spring, it has beautiful scarlet flowers with a central blotch of reddish brown. A cross between what Sweet termed the 'celandine-leaved stork's bill' (*P. fulgidum*) and the 'cow persnep-leaved stork's bill' (*P. lobatum*), *P.* Ardens was one of the many hybrids produced by James Lee (the younger) of the Hammersmith firm of Lee and Kennedy, a place whose size and fashionable reputation resulted in a mention in Thackeray's novel *Vanity Fair*. When Amelia offers her brother a kiss to thank him for a nosegay, the narrator interjects that 'for a kiss from such as dear creature as Amelia, I would purchase all Mr Lee's nurseries out of hand'.[10] What garden centre today would warrant such a complement?

Lee was not the only breeder to be attracted by the vivid scarlet flowers of *P. fulgidum*; along with the shrubby *P. cucullatum*, it was the most popular species for hybridizing at this time, not least in the creation of a group known as Uniques.[11] While *cucullatum* has continued to

Pelargonium x Ardens, Woottens Nursery, Wenhanston, Suffolk, 2010.

Pelargonium fulgidum.
Plate no. 69 in
Robert Sweet,
Geraniaceae. Engraving
by J. Watts after
drawing by Edwin
Dalton Smith.

flourish – due to the ongoing popularity of the Regal group (known in the United States as Martha Washingtons and in Germany as Edels) – *fulgidum*, which has a relatively short flowering period, has fallen out of flavour. In the 1820s, however, breeders had different priorities. The creation of the perfect vivid red was one of Colt Hoare's five great ambitions (his other experiments focused on purple, spotted, streaked and large-flowered varieties), and among his most successful *fulgidum* crosses were those he named Ignescens (fiery) and Scintillans (sparkling). A whole host of subtly different culti-vars followed on their heels.[12] Two from volume I of Sweet's *Geraniaceae* – 'Daveyanum' (a descendant of Ignescens' for which Thomas Davey's

P. Macranthon and P. Daveyanum, plate 469, illustrating 'Pelargonion', in *Dictionnaire
pittoresque d'histoire naturelle et des phénomènes de la nature.*

Kings Road nursery asked five guineas) and Robert Jenkinson's 'large
flowered stork's bill' (*P.* 'Macranthon') – are illustrated, in a suitably
elegant setting, in Guérin-Meneville's *Dictionnaire pittoresque d'histoire
naturelle* (1833–9).[13] Neither hybrid still exists.

The breeding, and housing, of so many tender plants depended
upon the development of greenhouses or conservatories (the terms

were interchangeable at the time).[14] Buildings with transparent roofs had first appeared at the end of the eighteenth century, when Humphry Repton noted that that 'the numerous tribe of geraniums, ericas and other exotic plants, requiring more light' had 'caused a very material alteration in the construction of the greenhouse'.[15] 'Heated by a fireplace that sent hot air through serpentine flues built into a back wall', these buildings were ideally suited to Cape plants – banksias, proteas and ericas as well as pelargoniums – whose primary requirements are good ventilation and a dry, moderate heat.[16] Most of these species would fall out of favour by the middle of the century when new steam and hot-water heating systems produced a humid atmosphere more conducive to the latest orchids and ferns. The only Cape plant to retain its popularity would be the pelargonium, whose adaptability to pot life, ease of reproduction, winter bloom, and often scented leaves rendered it unsackable.

But there was more to the new glasshouses than functionality. While Cobbett emphasised the '*moral* effects naturally attending a green-house', for most, a well-designed conservatory, attached 'to some room in the mansion', was among the 'refinements of modern

'Forcing Garden in Winter', from Humphry Repton, *Fragments on the Theory and Practice of Landscape Gardening* (London, 1816), coloured lithograph.

luxury'.[17] Once again *Vanity Fair* observes the trend. Imagining life as 'country-gentleman's wife' on £5,000 a year, Thackeray's most acute social critic, Becky Sharp, identifies the conservatory as a site and a symbol of desultory recreation. 'I could dawdle about in the nursery, and count the apricots on the wall', she muses. 'I could water plants in a greenhouse, and pick off dead leaves from the geraniums.'[18] Throughout the nineteenth century, picking leaves off a 'genteel geranium' was to remain a major activity for ladies of too much leisure.[19]

Not every Victorian novelist was as coolly unimpressed by the allure of the glass house. George Eliot's *The Mill on the Floss* (1860), and Charles Dickens's *David Copperfield* (1850) – novels also set in the 1820s – use it as a setting for lovers' trysts, for geranium-induced intoxication and moral danger.[20]

The Mill on the Floss is a novel about the struggle between duty and impulse, the obligations of the past and the promise of the future. One version of that contention involves Maggie Tulliver and Stephen Guest, who are strongly attracted to each other, although also attached to other people. The 'Great Temptation' builds for some time – and even survives a walk though the fashionable laburnums – until one evening, at a ball in his family mansion, Stephen invites Maggie to accompany him to the conservatory. The place is defined by its beguiling fakery. Maggie immediately notes the 'strange and unreal' effects that the artificial lighting creates on the plants: 'they look as if they belonged to an enchanted land . . . I could fancy they were all made of jewels.'

> She was looking at the tier of geraniums as she spoke, and Stephen made no answer; but he was looking at her – and does not a supreme poet blend light and sound into one, calling darkness mute, and light eloquent? Something strangely powerful there was in the light of Stephen's long gaze, for it made Maggie's face turn towards it and look upward at it – slowly, like a flower at the ascending brightness.[21]

They walk 'unsteadily on' until, as they come to the end of the conservatory, a 'mad impulse' overcomes Stephen and he showers Maggie's arm with kisses. Insulted, she transforms herself again, this time into a 'wounded war-goddess'. Maggie's blooming had been temporary, a product of 'forcing' in that peculiarly natural yet unnatural environment. Stephen is a good match for the jewel-like hothouse plants. He is first introduced by his 'diamond ring, attar of roses, and air of nonchalant leisure', but these, Eliot tells us, 'are the graceful and odoriferous result of the largest oil-mill and the most extensive wharf' in town. Maggie struggles but eventually resists the seductive odours of Stephen and money, and as she does so, another flower is evoked. Her story ends in drowning; as she and her brother Tom are swept up by the river whose power the mill and wharf exploit. But before this happens Maggie and Tom are given one last 'supreme moment', in which they live 'through again' the childhood in which they had 'roamed the daisied fields together'.[22]

The clear opposition that exists between the innocent daisies of childhood and the seductive geraniums of maturity is absent in *David Copperfield*, a novel largely concerned with confusions of identity. At the beginning of the story David's mother, Clara Copperfield, is a widow. We are told that she's charming but 'childish', a 'Baby' who cares more about looking good than about looking after her son. She wears 'pretty dresses' and displays a 'famous geranium' in the 'parlor-window'. Dickens does not say whether Clara Copperfield herself gives the plant much attention or whether that task too is delegated to the family's servant, another Clara, Clara Peggotty – a woman who likes to 'clean everything over and over again'. In any case, it is David's mother who takes advantage of the showy blossoms. One Sunday, Mr Murdstone, the mysterious 'gentleman' who has been pursuing her, walks the family home from church.

> He came in, too, to look at a famous geranium we had, in the parlor-window. It did not appear to me that he took much notice of it, but before he went he asked my mother to give

him a bit of the blossom. She begged him to choose it for himself, but he refused to do that — I could not understand why — so she plucked it for him, and gave it into his hand. He said he would never, never, part with it any more; and I thought he must be quite a fool not to know that it would fall to pieces in a day or two.[23]

David Copperfield was Freud's favourite novel and reading this scene one can understand why. If young Davy fails consciously to 'understand' what it is going on and to recognize his feelings for his mother, his subconscious has created a direct association between geraniums and desire. It is a pity then that when he next encounters the plants it is at the height of his infatuation with the 'enchanting' Dora Spenlow. He visits her in suburban Norwood, where she takes him to inspect the family's new greenhouse.

It contained quite a show of beautiful geraniums. We loitered along in front of them, and Dora often stopped to admire this one or that one, and I stopped to admire the same one, and Dora laughing, held the dog up childishly, to smell the flowers; and if we were not all three in Fairyland, certainly *I* was. The scent of a geranium leaf, at this day, strikes me with a half comical, half serious wonder as to what change has come over me in a moment; and then I see a straw hat and blue ribbons, and a quantity of curls, and a little black dog being held up, in two slender arms, against a bank of blossoms and bright leaves.[24]

'I Fall Into Captivity' is the chapter's title, but it is a fall that might have been predicted. Dora among the geraniums – a combination of 'curls' and 'blossoms', a childlike woman who poses among the plants without tending them – repeats Clara Copperfield precisely.

But all is not yet lost. While *The Mill on the Floss* offered a tragic perspective on growing up, Dickens gives his hero – one of whose many nicknames is 'Daisy' – a chance to mature and break his floral compulsion. Dora dies (the 'blossom withered in its bloom'), enabling David to marry again, and better. Sensible and domestically competent, Agnes is much more than a decorative flower and yet, as Amy King notes, Dickens insists that she too has a 'sweet blooming' side.[25]

Thrice Itself Through Power of Art

The suburban greenhouse so prized by the Spenlow family was a sign of the times. In 1824 J. C. Loudon published the first *Greenhouse companion* arguing that what had been a 'luxury' 50 years earlier had, due to the invention of cast iron, 'now become an appendage to every villa, and to many town residences'.[26] A handbook was needed, Loudon claimed, because the occupants of those residences were not yet familiar with the 'general maxims of exotic culture'.[27] And it was not only exotic plants about which the burgeoning urban middle class required tuition. What about positioning flower beds? Choosing shrubs? Maintaining a lawn? Loudon addressed these, and many other, issues in a series of instructional books which, along with those of his wife Jane, became 'the bibles of nineteenth-century gardeners'.[28] In 1826, he also founded the *Gardener's Magazine*, which ran until his death in 1843, and which set the trend for a whole range of other magazines, including the *Journal of Horticulture*, *Cottage Gardener* and 'the century's major gardening paper', Joseph Paxton's *Gardener's Chronicle*. Although *Curtis's Botanical Magazine* continued, and was imitated by the cheaper *Floral Magazine*, emphasis had shifted from the botanical and decorative to the practical and horticultural.[29] The purpose of most publications was 'the diffusion of useful knowledge' and diminutive wood-cuts were generally all that was offered by way of illustration.

Loudon's most influential work, *The Suburban Gardener and Villa Companion* (1838), included every type of garden from the 'First Rate' (over ten acres) to the 'Fourth Rate' (tucked behind the terraced houses of artisans and clerks; we might think of Mr Pooter, a little later, with his 'nice little back garden' and his 'capital little book' on gardening).[30] Loudon's great democratizing theme was that 'all the necessities of life may be obtained in a great perfection by the occupier of a suburban residence in the neighbourhood of London, who possesses £200 or £300 a year, as by the greatest noblemen in England, and a mere fraction of the expense.'[31] It's an idea that still governs journalism today, with its insistence that vast gardens provide ideas which can be scaled down. And the scaling down has no end. In 1838, greenhouses were still very expensive. Loudon estimated their cost at around £150–£200 (that is, the annual salary of many readers) and therefore suggested that a small heated pit might be sufficient to occupy clerical workers 'who have an hour or two to spare in the mornings and evenings'. In the 'smallest' houses, he proposed adding a two-foot bay to an ordinary window to create an aquarium-like 'plant cabinet' as 'an allusion to the green-house of the villa, or the conservatory of the mansion'.[32] The next step down in aspirational miniaturization was the window box or flower pot.

Glasshouses became more affordable both to private householders and to commercial growers after taxes on glass and brick were repealed (in 1845 and 1850 respectively). The new bounty of geraniums could be fully exploited, especially as the growing railway network enabled widespread distribution and therefore encouraged mass production. The bedding system – the practice of planting out greenhouse-reared plants during the summer and, for many, the epitome of the High Victorian garden – was both a consequence and a celebration of those changes. Bedding was a labour-intensive form of gardening but it was labour, as much as flora, that was on conspicuous display in urban front gardens, municipally run cemeteries, public botanical gardens and parks (all of which developed in the midnineteenth century). During the summer of 1859, for example, it was estimated that between 30,000 and 40,000 bedding plants had been planted in Hyde Park.[33] The head gardener at Waddesdon Manor, home of Ferdinand de Rothschild, famously claimed that you could judge a man's status by the size of his bedding order: '10,000 plants for a squire, 20,000 for a baronet, 30,000 for an Earl, and 50,000 for a Duke, but Waddesdon had 60,000.'[34]

The work of bedding had many facets. It was not simply that frost-tender plants had to be nurtured for eight months before anyone even saw them. It was not even that the plants had to be 'either of the same kind, or of the same general appearance' and had to 'flower at the same time'. Nor that they were to be planted so close together 'as to cover the beds by the middle of July'. Nor even that every autumn everything had to be dug up and every spring a whole new flower garden created. The labour intensified during the season itself, as gardeners were required to maintain continual vigilance over every aspect of the display. Dead leaves and faded blooms had to be removed

'Garden Work – Bedding out in June', *The Graphic* (4 June 1870).

as soon as they appeared and, the books instructed, 'any shoots that rise above six inches from the bed should be cut off or pegged down'.[35] The lawn in which the beds were situated was also to be kept smooth and daisy-free. The key word was 'trim'.[36]

Trimness emphasized the fact that, as Repton had argued, a garden belongs to 'art rather than to nature'.[37] In Loudon's version, the distinction translated into one between the picturesque, which imitated 'nature in a wild state', and the gardenesque, which imitated nature 'subjected to a certain degree of cultivation or improvement, suitable to the wants and wishes of man'.[38] Geraniums were the gardenesque epitomized. For one thing, they adapted well to pot life, which, Loudon noted approvingly, 'always checks and counteracts the natural habit of the plant'.[39] Pots were portable, and therefore changeable. They could also be lined up to create a 'simple and beautiful' effect 'in keeping with the formality' of neo-classical suburban villas and the newly introduced Italianate terraces of grander buildings.[40] Urns of scarlet geraniums placed at regular intervals are an invariable feature of the mid-century stately English gardens depicted by E. Adveno Brooke.

An important distinction between the picturesque and the gardenesque concerned the use of colour. Picturesque gardens mixed up flowers to create a 'broken and intricate' mixture of shades.[41] From the 1820s, however, a case began to be made for 'one beautiful colour': 'we do not, in general', wrote Leigh Hunt, 'love and honour any one single colour enough'. Hunt argued that as nature operated in blocks of blue (the sky) or brown (the fields), flowers should be massed to create a single 'pure' effect.[42] If nature could also be evoked to explain the choice of emphatically coloured flowers from the hot climates of South Africa (pelargonium, lobelia) and South America (verbena, calceolaria, salvia), it was, however, largely forgotten in the endeavour to make their colours (purple, blue, white, yellow and scarlet) even more emphatic. The 'purpose of nature', it seemed, was not to 'produce beautiful flowers, but fertile ones'.[43] Beauty was the task of floriculture and horticulture.

E. Adveno Brooke, 'The Parterre, Harewood House', in *The Gardens of England* (1856–7), colour-printed lithograph.

E. Adveno Brooke, 'Upper and Lower Terrace Gardens, Bowood', in *The Gardens of England* (1856–7), colour-printed lithograph.

For the first time, the careful arrangement of colours became an essential part of gardening. New interest in the physics of perception, colour theory and, in particular, colour wheels drew attention to questions of 'complementary' effects, and primary versus secondary colours. Goethe had argued that in order to achieve a sense of 'harmony' or 'completeness', the eye 'demands' a 'union' between a primary colour and its 'compound' (a mixture of the other two primaries).[44] Red, 'the most exciting and positive of all colours', was therefore best seen against 'its complementary green, the most soothing and grateful to the eye'. For Leigh Hunt, 'a geranium shining with its scarlet tops in the sun, the red of it being the more red for a back-ground of lime-trees' said nothing less than 'Paint me!'[45] The bedding system allowed the extension of this contrast into the garden where the grass's green set off large beds of scarlet geraniums. These were as much admired in literature as in life. In the opening sections of Coventry Patmore's *The Angel in the House*, for example, the lovers spend a 'sweet hour' admiring the lawn,

> Close-cut, and, with geranium-plots,
> A rival glow of green and red;[46]

And even in 'decay and death' (as geraniums often were after summer rain) the 'flaming clumps upon the shaven lawn', wrote S. W. Partridge, 'lends colour to the scene'.[47]

The proper display of colour relied on formal control. Bedding plants were carefully arranged according to geometrical designs within a single bed or in a number of symmetrically arranged beds. These were often circular but gardeners also experimented with crescents, commas and kidney- or s-shapes, whose colour effects – 'scarlet, crimson, blue, orange; masses of blossom lying on the greensward' – were generally best appreciated from an elevated terrace or upstairs window.[48] Bedding-out was also adopted by, and gradually came to be associated with, the new public parks of the mid- to late nineteenth century. There, other fashions developed: 'ribbon' borders, long narrow strips arranged in rows of red, white and blue, which were said to keep pedestrians on the move; circular 'pincushion' beds which featured floral dots of repeating colours; and 'carpet' bedding in which intricate emblems or words were represented.[49] Magazines and books gave detailed instructions on how to plan and fill these beds. In March 1863, for example, *Cottage Gardener* provided a complete list of the plants featured in the parterre at Straffan House, near Dublin. Twenty-five different geraniums of all styles and colours were added, with occasional 'nutmeg' or 'cinnamon' varieties included to provide scent.[50]

In search of contrast, gardeners began to introduce the 'neutral tints' of foliage-plants into the bed and 'brilliant edgings to define it'.[51] They also experimented with height, perhaps by creating a mound or by introducing a taller plant, such as a standard fuchsia, at the centre of a bed.[52] The editor of *The Floral World*, Shirley Hibberd, became famous for his geranium pyramid – a six-foot cone of rubble and chicken wire, thickly planted to give 'an even mass of dark horse-shoe foliage and brilliant scarlet flowers'.[53] Examples of all of these trends can still be found in public, if not usually private, gardens. I recently came across a plastic pyramid filled with red and white geraniums and purple petunias on the outskirts of Ipswich.

The bedding craze provided a new impetus to horticultural breeders. Pelargoniums – 'such obedient and plastic things' – had long been considered the perfect raw material for cultivation.[54] In *The Angel in the House*, Patmore described the 'pink or rose' geranium as 'thrice itself through power of art' and hoped that, analogously, his own 'happy skill' might cultivate 'new fairness' in the 'fair heart' of his beloved.[55] Initially, hybridization was seen as a rather genteel art. In 1824, Loudon had recommended that ladies try suspending nosegays of geranium blossoms above their conservatory plants to see what new varieties might result. The seedlings could then be passed on to a local nurseryman to develop. Mary Russell Mitford raised so many and of such quality that she was able to exchange hers for other plants, her 'only extravagance'.[56] But most cultivation took place on a much larger scale. The pelargonium gained a reputation, as Cobbett had noted, as

Geraniums and castor oil plants (*Ricinus communis*) planted in matching comma-shaped beds, Pollock House, Glasgow, 2011.

a new and rather grand type of 'florist's flower', grown for show and competition (according to strict criteria) between specialist growers; the first Pelargonium Society was established in 1842.[57] Florists were interested in any 'novelty of colour' and form. Petals were selected for their pansy-like blotches (to produce 'spotted' or 'French' varieties) or to be overlapping and circular, 'with perfectly smooth edges, as if stamped out' (for 'Fancy' cultivars).[58] The ambition was 'perfection', which seemed to mean something as different from its parents as possible.[59] As the 'stamped out' metaphor suggests, no one talked much about nature any more.

While the florist's cultivars dazzled on the exhibition bench, they weren't really suitable for garden use. Nor, really, was the long-established Unique type of pelargonium; it might perform beautifully in the shelter of the conservatory but 'as a bedding plant, it lacks bloom in the latter part of the season.'[60] The ideal bedder had to be more robust. It would bloom as brightly in August as in June, grow quickly but then stay compact, have bright flowers and leaves, and withstand the summer rain as well as heat. And, mostly, it would be red. In

Geranium pyramid on the outskirts of Ipswich, 2011.

Shirley Hibberd, 'Geranium Pyramid in the Author's Garden, Stoke Newington', *The Floral World* (July 1864).

search of such a paragon, breeders turned to the 'garden geranium' (*P. x hortorum*) first described in 1732, and noted, on 16 June 1819, as 'common' throughout Hampshire.[61] These plants resulted from crosses between *P. inquinans* – the red-flowered occupant of Rubens Peale's pot – and the horseshoe-leaved *P. zonale*. Both were tall, shrubby species and most early 'zonals' such as 'Frogmore Scarlet' were not particularly successful bedders. A step forward came when a Frogmore was accidentally fertilized by the ivy-leaved geranium with which it shared a basket. The resulting plant combined the colour and leaf of the zonal with the low growing habit of the ivy and was named 'Tom Thumb' after the popular American dwarf performer. Within a short period, the zonal geranium was established as 'the king of bedding plants' and in 1861, Donald Beaton, head gardener at Shrubland Park and 'flower garden' editor of *Cottage Gardener*, declared that his 'new order of seedlings' was so impressive that it would soon be time to 'drown all the bedding Geraniums that existed in 1855 in the bottom of the Thames'.[62] Beaton specialized in narrow-flowered 'Nosegay' varieties (whose parentage included 'an old inhabitant of our greenhouses', a very early hybrid known as *P. forthergillii*), but most hybridization focused on zonals.[63] Every random mutation represented the possibility of a breakthrough. The next decade saw the development of 'ornamental-foliaged' or 'fancy leaved' varieties, the most popular of which was Peter Grieve's tri-coloured 'Mrs Pollock' and, for many, the icing on the cake, double-flowered varieties such as Victor Lemoine's 'Glorie de Nancy'.[64] The French had come relatively late to the geranium craze – in 1835, Frances Trollope, visiting Paris, concluded that 'the cultivation of this lovely race, and the production of a new variety in it, is not a matter of so great an interest in France as in England' – but Lemoine was to become one of the greatest of all breeders.[65] He developed dwarf zonals, ivy-leaved varieties and, in 1892, the most famous of scarlet geraniums, 'Paul Crampel'. For a long time, the bedding plant of choice in the Buckingham Palace flower beds (where it was thought to match the colour of the guardsmen's tunics), 'Paul Crampel' was described by the filmmaker Derek

Jarman, a hundred years after its creation, as 'the true scarlet, the one and only colour of a geranium'.[66]

But all that was still to come. In introducing 'Madame Lemoine' in 1868, *The Floral Magazine* was already weary:

> We have recorded so many strange results in the family of Pelargoniums in our pages already, that the appearance of a double-flowering variety is not so much a matter of astonishment. We have seen great changes produced in the colouring of the leaf, in the form, size, and colour of the flower; and now we have the increase in the number of petals sufficient to form a double flower.[67]

Pelargoniums had become 'so varied in habit and colour', noted Hibberd, that 'with geraniums alone a skilful artist can produce almost any effect that may be required'.[68] There was now no excuse for a bed full of 'trashy Tom Thumbs purchased at three shillings a dozen'.[69]

Amid the excitement of all this hybridization, it was no wonder that Charles Darwin took an interest. He found a rich resource for the exploration of variation, mutation, fertility, inheritance and the 'gradual and accumulative force of selection' in the breeders' reports which appeared in journals like *Gardener's Chronicle* and *Cottage Gardener*, and which he often followed up in correspondence.[70] *On the Origin of Species* (1859) had simply noted the notoriously 'complicated' crosses achieved with *Pelargonium* and that 'many of these hybrids seed freely', but during the 1860s Darwin was able to explore the 'practical experiments of horticulturalists' further.[71] He learned that 'Queen Mab' and 'Alba Multiflora' could withstand great heat and concluded that they 'must have a widely different constitution than most other varieties of this plant'. He observed that variegation (which seemed to be associated with dwarfing) depended on soil type. Donald Beaton reported that in six years of raising 20,000 seedlings of 'Punch' in Suffolk, none had variegated leaves; when the same variety was grown in Surrey,

P. 'Mrs Pollock', *The Floral Magazine*, vol. 11 (1862), plate 101. Illustration by Vincent Brooks.

377

P. 'Madame Lemoine', *The Floral Magazine*, vol. VII (1868), plate 377.

however, a third were variegated. Subtle changes in soil type and temperature also had an effect on fertility. Darwin was interested to read that *P. fulgidum* – the 1820s cultivator's favourite – had become sterile unless, that is, the seed was overwintered in a dry stove.[72]

But it was 'peloric' pelargonium cultivars – whose regular round-petals were so favoured by competitive florists – that most intrigued Darwin as he thought about reversion and inheritance. In their symmetrical arrangement, he noted, the peloric flowers of a variety such as 'Queen of Scarlet' resembled those of a geranium, yet, in having some infertile stamens, they were more like an erodium. Perhaps, Darwin speculated, the cultivar had 'reverted to the state of some primordial form, the progenitor of the three closely related genera'.[73]

Geranium-Coloured

On 31 October 1794 members of the Manchester Literary and Philosophical Society gathered to hear a lecture by a young chemist called John Dalton. Dalton was the first to describe, and offer an explanation for, the phenomenon of colour blindness. He detailed his own confusions between the colour of sealing wax and a laurel leaf, between mud and a ribbon that others said was scarlet, and was particularly surprised to observe that the flowers of a 'horseshoe cranesbill' (*P. zonale*) which appeared 'sky-blue' to him in daylight, was 'very near yellow, but with a tincture of red' when seen by candlelight. About ten years later, magazines began to use 'geranium' to designate a fashionable colour.[74]

Although the plants themselves came in every shade from white to deep purple, 'geranium' referred quite precisely to a shade of red with a 'flat' concentration not often found in nature and, as Ruskin noted in 1870 in his *Lectures on Art*, difficult to reproduce in paint. Since 'the brightness of the hue dazzled the eye' and disguised the form, Ruskin presented his students with a drawing of 'a single cluster of the scarlet geranium, in mere light and shade'. 'I think you will feel that its domed form, and the flat lying of the petals one over the

'Scarlet Geranium',
1875, George Allen,
engraving and
mezzotint on wove
paper, after drawing
by John Ruskin.

other, in the vaulted roof of it, can be seen better thus than if they
had been painted scarlet.'[75]

Ruskin was not the only one who thought geraniums would be
better without the geranium colour. For many, the flower had become
a badge of *arriviste* flamboyance. In 1843, William Thackeray, never
reluctant to make a dig at his rival Charles Dickens, wrote to a friend
after attending a ball: 'How splendid Mrs Dickens was in pink satin
and Mr Dickens in geraniums and ringlets.'[76] Geraniums were only to
be expected of a man whose work, in Ruskin's eyes, was spoiled by
'brilliant exaggeration'.[77] But Dickens wasn't put off by this kind of
comment. According to his daughter Mamie, he 'loved all flowers,
but especially bright flowers, and scarlet geraniums were his favourite
of all'.[78] Thackeray's comment probably refers to the sprig he wore in

Geranium buttonhole, made and photographed by Sharon Willoughby.

his buttonhole and which made him, like Tom Pinch in *Martin Chuz-zlewit*, 'very smart and summerlike for the day'.[79] (He never went as far as the Major in *Dombey and Son*, who 'wore a whole geranium in his buttonhole.'[80]) Once, after a reading in Dublin, fans mounted the stage and gathered the fallen petals as keepsakes.[81]

Dickens didn't stop there. He used geraniums in his dinner-table decorations, grew them in his conservatory and planted up great scarlet beds at his home at Gad's Hill. His daughter Katie told him, 'Papa, I think when you are an angel your wings will be made of looking-glasses and your crown of scarlet geraniums.'[82] While his crown remains a matter of uncertainty, scarlet geraniums certainly festooned his coffin.[83] It seems odd that, although one can still buy a salmon-rose cultivar called 'Little Dorritt' and the fancy-leaved 'Dolly Varden' (named after the red-ribboned coquette in *Barnaby Rudge*), no one – not even the Dickens Fellowship, whose members wear a red geranium badge – has yet produced a 'Dickens' variety. 'Tennyson', on the other hand, is a rather fancy crimson and white cultivar; presumably a homage to the poet's 'Now Sleeps the Crimson Petal'

(1847). But while the Poet Laureate was said to have enjoyed the way the red potted geraniums on his terrace framed the view of the blue Sussex hills, his poetry consistently rejects 'squares of tropic summer' in favour of the 'meanest weed' and 'vilest herb that runs to seed / Beside its native fountain'.[84]

And it wasn't only Tennyson who looked to the domesticated exotic for a symbol of a 'brassy' and over-reaching age. In 1843, Nathaniel Hawthorne wrote a story about a mad scientist who, believing in 'man's ultimate control over nature', sets about removing his beautiful wife's birthmark with the same concoction that had removed 'unsightly blotches' from the leaves of his geranium. She drinks his potion but, as her birthmark vanishes, the 'now perfect woman' dies.[85]

'Walking dress' with 'velvet spencer of bright geranium', *Belle assemblée, being Bell's Court and Fashionable Magazine* (December 1819).

George C. Leighton,
'Charles Dickens
giving a reading'.

If Hawthorne's parable suggests that science must hold back from correcting nature's imperfection, for Ruskin and his followers, it was science not nature that produced imperfection. The problem of hybridization was not the removal of a blighted leaf but the creation of a race of Frankenstein's monsters – 'unfortunate beings, pampered and bloated above their natural size, stewed and heated into diseased growth; corrupted by evil communication into speckled and inharmonious colours'.[86] Moreover, their use in the bedding system spoke eloquently of their means of production, for nature's creatures were treated like factory products, existing as disposable 'mere masses of colour' rather than as 'an assemblage of living beings', each of whose entire life deserved careful attention.[87] Even Shirley Hibberd, who had once advised readers on geranium pyramids, began to rail against the taste of 'savages', suggesting that a scarlet bed was like 'the blazing fire at the mouth of a coal pit'. What kind of 'training ground for mind and morals' could such a garden provide?[88]

And if bedding was 'unnatural in feeling', it was also 'ugly in effect'.[89] The 'ugliness that has covered all modern life' was an irresistible theme, and geraniums were counted among the most insidious perpetrators. In a 1879 lecture on 'Making the Best of It', for example, William Morris launched a by-then familiar attack on the 'over-artificiality' of various commercial hybrids, 'inventions of men' rather than nature, but he reserved particular venom for the 'scarlet geranium' – a 'bad colour altogether', which demonstrated that 'even flowers can be thoroughly ugly'.[90] It was a view Oscar Wilde seemed to share. Contemplating the afterlife, he wondered if he might end up in a heaven that was 'gold and purple and fire' (like a Fra Angelico painting) or whether he would come back to life as a flower. It wouldn't be the Pre-Raphaelite lily, however; 'perhaps for my sins,' he joshed, 'I shall be made a red geranium!!' – a flower, that is, with 'no soul'.[91]

Socialist attacks on the alienation of industrial mass culture were sometimes hard to distinguish from simple snobbery about that culture's consumers. In 1862, Andrew Murray, Assistant Secretary of the new Royal Horticultural Society, wrote anonymously to the *Gardener's Chronicle* denouncing the 'gaudy glitter' of Joseph Paxton's bedding displays for the Crystal Place, which after the Great Exhibition of 1851 had relocated to suburban Sydenham. According to Murray, Paxton's beds (some of which even mimicked different kinds of butterflies) were designed to appeal to the 'lower elements of our taste': 'it is the savage who is caught by the gayest colours, and a liking for them and personal ornament is a remnant of primitive barbarism'.[92] The language had slipped. Red was no longer simply a 'primitive' (that is, primary) colour, it was the colour of primitivism. A similar metaphorical elision occurred with the notion of the 'showy masses'.[93]

By the end of the century, the association of bright colour with the 'lower element' of taste had been firmly established. It was perfectly acceptable for the poor to like red, as Octavia Hill told the Kyrle Society in 1884. 'Till you stay a little in the colourless, forlorn desolation of the houses in the worst courts, till you have lived among the monotonous, dirty tints of the poor districts of London, you little know what the colours of your curtains, carpets, and wall-papers are to you.'[94] But if, as Hill said, 'all bright colour exhilarates and gives a sense of gladness', why couldn't everyone enjoy it? Because, it seemed, sophisticated tastes were more inclined to 'complex' tertiary colours like olive or russet. What was exhilarating in the pauper's garret was simply a 'glare' anywhere else. In *Tess of the d'Urbervilles* (1891), Thomas Hardy uses the image of a misplaced geranium to make it clear that the brand new d'Urberville manor is hardly a 'manorial house in the ordinary sense'. It might look well enough in its immediate setting – 'acres of green-houses' and a 'bright thriving and well-kept garden' – but set against the wider landscape, the manor's 'rich-red' brick is like a 'geranium bloom against the subdued colours around'. The forest that surrounds the house is not just any forest, of course; it is 'one of the few remaining woodlands in England of primaeval date wherein Druidical mistletoe was still to be found on aged oaks'.[95] The contrast couldn't be greater: on the one hand, antiquity and druidical mistletoe; new money and red geraniums, on the other. No one spoke any longer of geraniums as 'rich gifts from other climes'.[96] African plants had been 'torn from the soil which they loved, and of which they were the spirit and the glory' to be placed 'in earth that they know not'. Surely they would be happier growing 'wild and free' – back home. Get rid of the 'tenants', became the rallying cry; give back the garden to 'our sweet old border flowers'.[97]

four

The Geranium in the Window

And I love – how I love – the plants that fill
The pots on my dust-dry window sill –
    A sensitive sickly crop.
Austin Dobson, 'A City Flower', 1864

Context is all in the language of flowers. At the very moment that large beds of scarlet geraniums came to symbolize the ugly uniformity of industrial mass culture, the single straggly potted geranium was co-opted for a brave last stand against that culture's encroachment. Home was the refuge and, if Victorian fiction is anything to go by, at the heart of the home was the pot plant. The plant and its container set the scene and even, sometimes, propelled the story.

Of all homes, the 'cottage with bright, transparent windows showing pots full of blooming balsams or geraniums' increasingly became the ideal, a sign of both the 'trim, cheerful' countryside and of a contented family life.[1] Like the cat with which it was often pictured, the scarlet bloom in the window suggested that what lay within was homely and cheerful, 'clean and bright'.[2] A few pots were always included in the popular cottage genre paintings in which a family gathered in the parlour for a christening, a wedding breakfast or a funeral. Even 'news from the front' – in Alexander Rossi's 1899 painting – fails to disturb the glowing geraniums and glowing girlish cheeks. It became axiomatic that, as Flora Thompson put it, 'a well-whitened hearth, a home-made

Ralph Hedley, *Blinking in the Sun*, 1881, oil on canvas.

rag rug in bright colours, and a few geraniums on the window-sill would cost nothing, but made a great difference to the general effect.' By 1939, when Thompson published *Lark Rise to Candleford*, rosy visions of rural life had become so pervasive that George Sturt felt the need to assert that, certainly as he remembered life in a Surrey village, it wasn't 'an idyll of samplers and geraniums in cottage windows'.[3] For the most part, the rustic cottage of art and literature was a product of the urban imagination.

'Potting Geraniums'. Photograph by George Woods, East Sussex, *c.* 1890.

Alexander Rossi, *News from the Front*, 1899, oil on canvas.

The population shift from the countryside to the city that had begun in Europe during the eighteenth century accelerated dramatically over the course of the next hundred years. Britain was in the vanguard of urbanization and much of the early writing about its consequences came from experiences of London, whose population swelled from one to seven million over the course of the century, and of the industrial cities of Glasgow, Manchester and Liverpool. By 1850, around 54 per cent of the population of England and Wales lived in towns and cities, with nearly 14 per cent in London. By 1900, urban dwellers constituted nearly 75 per cent of the population.[4]

Most inhabitants of cities didn't have much access to gardens or even parks, at least until mid-century; but, in the poets' eyes, the 'burning instinct' of 'close-pent man' for some 'hint / That Nature lives' was 'inextinguishable'.[5] Venetians, with their particularly limited supply of land, were much admired for their ingenuity in finding places to grow all manner of plants. Parisians too were resourceful. Before the Revolution, 'amateur horticulture' was illegal but its devotees, mainly artisans who worked from home, refused to give up their precariously arranged pots; when the government inspector passed by, they simply brought everything inside. Nothing, wrote Louis-Sébastien Mercier,

Geraniums in Venice, 2010.

Thomas Rowlandson, 'The Pot Seller', from *Cries of London* (1799), colour aquatint.

could stand in the way of a Parisian's desire to make an 'offering to the exiled goddesses Pomona and Flora'.[6] The 'love of a country life and growing things' were seen as synonymous and, in London, 'hyacinth-glasses in the parlour-window, and geranium-pots in the little front court' testified repeatedly to 'some dim remembrance of better things'.[7] Those without a glass or a pot, observed Thomas Fairchild, 'content our selves with a Nosegay rather than fail'.[8]

The Flower Market at Covent Garden. Engraved by E. Buchman from the painting by W. B. Gardner and hand-coloured.

W. D. Gardner Sc.

Writing in 1722, Fairchild was already complaining about the problems of smoke and lack of light, but the more difficult it became to grow things, it seemed, the greater the love of nature that was displayed. By the 1840s, the city dweller's residual 'love of flowers' had become an important theme in the anxious discourse of social and sanitary reform. The 1843 Parliamentary Committee on the Labouring Poor reported 'striking instances' in which the 'possession of an allotment' had been 'the means of reclaiming the criminal, reforming the dissolute, and of changing their whole moral character and conduct', while a later commentator broke off from considering 'female labour in the metropolis' to note how 'wonderful' it was 'to witness the love which the poorest and lowest people in London have for flowers'.

> They watch over their sickly geraniums and blighted dwarf rose-trees with more devotion than a gardener bestows on hot-house plants . . . This love of flowers is one of the most hopeful symptoms in the condition of the *very poor* in London.[9]

Many reformers tried to convince themselves – and the poor – that the solution to every problem from overcrowding to alcoholism to social unrest was a pot plant in the parlour window. But this wasn't a question of wanting poverty to be picturesque, of masking 'decay / With flowers': window gardening was promoted as a form of 'rational recreation'.[10] It was certainly rational to begin with something immediately observable – 'how much they seem to enjoy their bit of garden' – as the basis for the reformation of character. Allotments were valued partly because their cultivation was so time-consuming. As Samuel Broome reported to the National Association for the Promotion of Social Science, gardening 'fills up all their leisure hours of a morning and evening; they scarcely have time to smoke a pipe . . . Very rarely do you find a man who is fond of flowers taken up for a misdemeanor of any kind.'[11] Moreover, it was believed that if a gardener was given, or leased, his *own* little plot of soil, he would acquire an increased respect, and aspiration, for property. Window-gardening – increasingly thought of as women's work – did not fill up much time, but it was believed that by developing pride in her window box – that is, in her public face – a woman too would learn good habits. Caring for her pot plants, she would gradually acquire a 'taste' for, and be 'brought over' to, 'cleanliness, regularity, order, and self-respect' in every dimension of her private life.[12]

While any flower was better than none, a geranium had special qualities. For one thing, its association with cottage life made it an honorary native species – in the industrial city or even in an Indian hill station, it recreated a bit of 'home'. Moreover, the plants' uprooting and imprisonment in pots recalled the way their owners had been uprooted and imprisoned in tenement housing. A typical example is *Jenny and her Geranium*, a children's book set in 1840s London. We first meet the heroine as she stands in the 'dingy doorway of an old, rotting house' dreaming of 'pleasant cottages crowned with honeysuckle'. Her 'longing' is 'enhanced by the sight of a splendid geranium in full bloom in the window behind her, and on which she every now and then threw a loving and rapturous look'. If the plant could bloom 'in so arid a desert as Challoner's Court', the story implies, perhaps so too could Jenny.[13]

But survival was not the geranium's only task. Its much-vaunted brightness also came into play – as a kind of dirt-seeking searchlight. 'I must keep everything extra clean,' says the eponymous heroine of Harriet Boultwood's novel *Dot's Scarlet Geranium* (1890), 'or the geranium will make the room look dirty – the flower is so bright.'[14] The plant that had helped eighteenth-century aristocrats to combat their lassitude now provided an evangelical spur to working-class industry. In one German magazine story, a woman who is 'accustomed from sunrise to sunset to drudge on in the most degrading of services' finds herself so invigorated by the gift of a geranium that she arrives home with energy to spare and decides to wash the window – 'the filth upon it was in such contrast to the glowing geranium'. Improvement follows improvement, even her productivity at the

Jenny and her Geranium.   [Page 9.

factory increases, until she finally reaches the last dusty item in the room, her bible. 'How had God worked this miracle? It was but with a pot of geranium that a boy from the country had brought to her. That was all!'[15]

The intended benefits were not merely personal and moral. *Jenny and Her Geranium* ends when her neighbours too begin cultivating geraniums and are thus 'reclaimed from drunkenness'. House-pride, starting with pot-pride, ends up in neighbourhood-pride. In 'a world of general disorder', concludes the anonymous author, with a rather different metaphor, 'good example is catching'.[16] In the 1850s, George Godwin, editor of the influential reforming magazine *The Builder*, began to argue that new buildings should include ledges wide enough to contain window boxes.[17]

The Evangelical Geranium

Of the various philanthropic projects designed to promote window gardening, one of the most successful seems to have been that organized during the 1860s by the Revd Samuel Hadden Parkes, senior curate of St George's Bloomsbury. After observing the 'care and attention' with which some of his parishioners cultivated their plants, he decided that their 'latent taste' might be 'turned to better account' through the encouragement of a flower show.[18] In fact the taste was not so latent. Working-class flower shows were regularly staged by florists' organizations such as the Stoke Newington Chrysanthemum Society, founded in 1846, and the Tower Hamlets Floricultural Society, founded in 1859. But while these were run entirely by and for their members, the new scheme was simply '*for* the working classes' who were 'not expected to take any role other than as exhibitors'.[19] Everything was to be organized by the church, with the help of better-off local residents.

Ninety-four plants made it to the first show, held in Little Coram Street's Bible Mission Room in July 1860. The venture was reported, as an example of 'gardening under difficulties', in the *Journal of Horticulture and Cottage Gardener*, whose editors confessed that their initial thought was that a flower show confined to the working classes of Bloomsbury 'must be a joke – some satire upon our metropolitan shows, and that "Bloomsbury" was selected as an apt name for such a quiz'.[20] But it wasn't a joke – and the fame of the Bloomsbury show soon spread, especially after Lord Shaftesbury, an evangelical Conservative force behind numerous ameliorative reforms, became its figurehead. Shaftesbury's ideal was a 'stable and hierarchic society bound together by mutual obligations between rich and poor' and nothing in the Revd Parkes's published writing suggests that he thought otherwise.[21] But while it was often argued that 'the love of flowers' was 'a bond of union with all classes, rich and poor', that didn't mean that everyone was to love the *same* flowers. The model, as ever, was village life, whose annual fête demonstrated a 'communion', rather than a dissolving away, of 'classes' – 'orchids, delicately reared in heat, are gathered under one tent with the hardy wild flowers of the field . . . the question is, not which of these is more beautiful or better than its neighbour, but which is the best of its kind.'[22]

THE PRIZE GERANIUM. *(See p. 10.)*

After the first year, it was decided to limit the Bloomsbury competition to three categories – geranium, fuschia and annuals – there being no point in 'encouraging the poor to cultivate plants which cannot repay them for their trouble, and which must cause disappointment'.[23] Although one of the show's organizers expressed his disapproval at the reluctance of 'the poor' to buy or grow plants especially for exhibition, saying 'they will simply send any they may happen to have in their possession, and nine times out of ten those plants are Geraniums', Parkes was less interested in the plants themselves than in the care taken over them. The working-class members of the East End floricultural societies competed at a high level of horticultural expertise; the Bloomsbury show, however, was simply 'a means of cheering their lives and inducing habits of care, prudence and forethought'.[24]

Also cheering was the show's relocation to the private garden of Russell Square. 'The denizens of the square need not fear that any injury would be inflicted upon the trees or flowers growing within their palisaded enclosure,' insisted the *Journal of Horticulture and Cottage Gardener*, 'for the authorities at Kew and Crystal Palace will bear testimony in addition to our own that no such outrages are perpetrated in their gardens, not withstanding the unrestrained admission to them of the working classes.' The move to Russell Square made the show famous and Parkes was pleased to note that 'upwards of 3,000 persons, rich and poor together' attended.

> Of course . . . there were no new plants from China or Japan
> . . . no wondrous masses of pelargonium bloom like those
> of Fraser; but there was that which was more remarkable
> still, for there were plants grown in areas by domestic ser-
> vants; in the mews by the wives and children of stablemen;
> in the garrets by poor sempstresses; in kitchens by water-
> cress girls; in first and second floors by costermongers; in
> any imaginable nook and corner by the children of National
> and Ragged Schools, and one even in the sick ward of the
> parish workhouse.[25]

The flower show model of rich and poor together but apart, each content with their appropriate bloom, also formed the basis of an novel published in 1880 by the Religious Tract Society, *The Story of a Geranium; or, The Queen of Morocco*. As the title suggests, the pelargonium in question is no ordinary variety but a rare and expensive one – the kind that might be available from 'Fraser', John Fraser's prize-winning nursery in Leyton. The heroine is Susan, who lives in a 'neatly kept' cottage, waters her plants every evening, and never forgets a 'nosegay for the table'. 'We must not suppose,' the author tells us, 'that because Susan was a poor child, she had no taste to admire the beautiful works of God.' But that taste leads to trouble. One day, out shopping, Susan admires a liveried servant carrying a bundle of beautiful geranium cuttings tied together in wet moss. One falls from his hand but when she rushes to give it back, he's gone. There's nothing for Susan to do but take the cutting home. Under her care, it grows lustily and soon 'the petals of the flower looked just as if they were made of velvet; quite black in the middle, and softening off towards the edges into deep crimson. Susan thought she had never seen any flower so beautiful.' When the plant wins the Industrial School competition, Susan is not 'puffed up' by praise; which is lucky since, as soon as the judges recognize 'Queen of Morocco', a 'new and very scarce geranium', she is assumed to have stolen it and stripped of her prize. Susan's name is cleared, but she has to relinquish the plant to its original owner, Lady Walton. In its place, she's given 'a neat little stand' for her window and some 'pretty', that is, ordinary, geraniums to fill it. Everything's back in its place, nice and tidy.[26]

'Window Gardening
Flower Show', *The Graphic*
(November 1884).

Illustration from
*The Story of a Geranium;
or, The Queen of Morocco*
(London, 1880).

What was sometimes called the 'Bloomsbury movement', or even the 'Bloomsbury Floral Institution', gradually spread throughout London – in 1867, for example, the *Lancet* described a show in the grounds of the Middlesex Hospital in which pots cultivated by children on the wards competed against those grown on the window-sills of local 'very poor persons' – and by the end of the century, window-gardening initiatives could be found in many big cities, from Edinburgh to New York.[27] Even the Royal Horticultural Society introduced 'an Exhibition of Plants grown by the working classes of London' in its summer show. Every exhibitor would receive two tickets, prompting Revd Parkes to enthuse that 'it will be quite like a holiday to spend a day in the beautiful Gardens at South Kensington, almost as good as a trip to the country.'[28]

The Therapeutic Geranium

The efforts of Parkes and his associates drew upon, and fed into, evolving trends in sanitary reform during the 1860s and 1870s. While their general aim was the establishment of hygienic habits, their interest in plants was not simply a consequence of the fact that, as (Dr) Anton Chekhov observed, the 'smell of geranium and carbolic' so often went together.[29] Chekhov was presumably thinking of a scented-leaved geranium whose 'wholesome odours' were much in demand to mask bodily smells.[30] 'Attar of Roses', a popular cultivar of *P. capitatum*, was often placed in the bedroom and its leaves were a common ingredient in potpourris and scented sachets. 'It is strange,' noted Grant Thorburn, 'that a *green leaf*, plucked from a plant in no way similar, should possess all the flavour of the *flower* plucked from another.'[31] But rose was just one of the scents that geranium leaves were thought to mimic: every aroma from nutmeg, ginger and camphor to lemon, apple and peppermint seemed to emanate from one variety or another.

For many, however, the goal was not to disguise 'bad' air but to destroy it. Even as germ theory took hold in the 1850s and '60s, the miasmic theory of disease, which proposed a close connection between ill-health and inadequate ventilation, continued to exert an influence. For Parkes and his great mentor, George Godwin of *The Builder* magazine, many urban social ills could be traced back to 'pestilential miasma' and a 'want of pure air'. First came 'feelings of exhaustion and lowness of spirits, and these tempt the use of stimulants – the fruitful parents of all crime'. From there it was a short step to 'debility, continued fever, death, widowhood, orphanage, pauperism, and money-loss to the living'.[32] The simplicity of miasmic theory encouraged a belief in simple solutions: if the air was purified, perhaps the rest would also improve.

Mid-Victorian journalists commonly imagined urban plants as sharing a 'torpid life' with their owners in the 'musty courts and alleys' of a pathological city. In particular, the geranium featured as a kind of floral equivalent of a canary sent down the mine to see if there was any clean air at all. Sometimes its troubles were correlated with a specific problem, such as the introduction of a gas works: 'No improvement can ever reach the infected neighbourhoods', declared the *Illustrated London News* in 1864, 'no new streets, no improved dwellings, not even a garden is possible within a circle of at least a quarter of a mile in diameter, and not so much as a geranium can flourish in a window-sill.'[33] Most often, however, the problem, for people, as for their plant representatives, was simply the overcrowded, soot-filled city itself. In 1855, Shirley Hibberd lamented that 'thousands of beautiful plants are every spring and summer brought from the nurseries around London, and sold in the city to undergo the slow death of suffocation – dying literally from asphyxia, from the absorption of soot in the place of air.'[34]

Those plants which did survive asphyxiation were called on to diagnose a wide variety of diseases. The Christian Socialist Charles Kingsley argued that

> the sickly geranium which spreads its blanched leaves against the cellar panes, and peers up, as if imploringly, to the narrow slip of sunlight at the top of the narrow alley, had it a voice, could tell more truly than ever a doctor in the town, why little Bessy sickened of the scarlatina, and little Johnny of the hooping-cough, till the toddling wee things who used to pet and water it were carried off each and all of them one by one to the churchyard sleep.[35]

And if the leaves weren't allowed entirely to 'blanch', perhaps the geranium could also attempt a cure. Plant respiration, argued Parkes, adjusted the atmosphere to 'an average state of composition', according to 'the beautiful and wise law of compensation'.[36] While

'Mother with sick baby and geranium', a popular magazine illustration of 1899.

modern society ran on competitive and mechanistic lines, the law of nature, it was argued, was that of cooperation or, as John Ruskin put it in 1860, 'the Law of Help': 'The power which causes the several portions of the plant to help each other, we call life.'[37] Nine years later, in a lecture entitled 'The Two Breaths', Kingsley elaborated on the 'mutual dependence and mutual helpfulness' that existed between people and plants:

> The delicate surface of the green leaves absorbs the carbonic acid, and parts it into its elements, retaining the carbon to make woody fibre, and courteously returning you the oxygen to mingle with the fresh air, and be inhaled by your lungs once more. Thus do you feed the plants; just as the plants feed you; while the great life-giving sun feeds both; and the geranium standing in the sick child's window does not

merely rejoice his eye and mind by its beauty and freshness, but repays honestly the trouble spent on it; absorbing
the breath which the child needs not, and giving to him the
breath which he needs.[38]

The geranium provided, in miniature, the exchange of bad air
for good that many reformers, even as they came to abandon miasmic
theory, continued to believe was necessary for urban living. In fact,
the 'lungs of the city' argument doesn't make such sense, even when
larger green spaces such as parks are concerned. 'It takes about three
acres of woods to absorb as much carbon dioxide as four people exude
in breathing, cooking, and heating', Jane Jacobs noted a hundred
years later: 'the oceans of air circulating about us, not parks, keep
cities from suffocating.'[39]

In Kingsley's *Glaucus*, Little Bessy tries to combat her scarletina,
and Little Johnny his whooping cough, by tending their geranium,
but the virtuous trio are not in the end strong enough to counter the
pernicious influence of 'the father and mother' who try 'to supply by
gin that very vital energy which fresh air and pure water, and the
balmy breath of woods and heaths, were made by God to give':

> the little geranium did its best, like a heaven-sent angel, to
> right the wrong which man's ignorance had begotten, and
> drank in, day by day, the poisoned atmosphere, and formed
> it into fair green leaves, and breathed into the children's
> faces from every pore, whenever they bent over it, the life-
> giving oxygen for which their dulled blood and festered
> lungs were craving in vain.[40]

The Educational Geranium

Thousands of geraniums did their best to show up the dirt and clean
the air, and still more suffered ill-treatment – 'I tend too little, or too
much; / they die from want of skill' – so that slovenly housewives,

drunks, misers and, most often, careless-but-essentially-good children could be reformed.[41] They warned against laziness, boastfulness, lying and cheating. They encouraged nurturing and self-sacrifice. Most of the moral tales involved people behaving badly to a geranium, whose very stems, leaves and buds 'all seemed to reproach' them, but occasionally the geranium itself was naughty.[42] One particularly recalcitrant 'little slip' who 'didn't like her pot of earth' and 'said she wouldn't grow' was tied 'to a little stick' and placed in a 'very dark' closet until she straightened up and stopped being 'sulky'.[43]

The pot, made of vulnerable clay, provided another key protagonist. In Jennie Chappell's 'The Prize Geranium', the drama rests on a confusion between two pot plants competing in a Sunday School show. When Lottie's pot breaks, she substitutes her cousin Kate's and wins the prize. But 'why was it that no gush of pride and joy that instant gladdened her heart?' The prize is 'as wormwood' to Lottie, especially when she discovers that angelic Kate has suddenly become 'dangerously ill'. So she confesses and Kate recovers, happy both to receive her rightful prize and 'to comfort the penitent'. A graver sin is revealed in Mary Russell Day's novel *John Marriot's Idol; or, The Scarlet Geranium* (1888), the story of a single pot, the 'constant companion' of an old miser.[44] The problem, it turns out, is not that John idolizes his beautiful geranium, but that he's hiding someone else's money in its pot. When the terracotta breaks, all is revealed. The geranium was innocent, an unwilling dupe.

Perhaps the most multifaceted of shattered pot fables is that presented in chapter four of Edward Bulwer-Lytton's novel *The Caxtons* (1849). As 'The Broken Flower Pot', it was frequently reprinted, at least until the 1920s, as a stand-alone cautionary tale in magazines and in anthologies with such titles as *Ethics for Children*.[45] The story begins in the aftermath of a geranium mishap. Pisistratus, known as Sisty, has mischievously pushed a pot out of the window, little caring that his mother had 'reared' the plant herself nor that she cherished its 'dear, dear' container. So far so naughty, but little Sisty's redemption is soon underway. First he owns up that he did it, and not by accident, but 'for fun' and to see the look on his father's face. In fact, his confession inspires Papa to an even better look (one of admiration) and an adage: 'For truth, that blooms all the year round, is better than a poor geranium; and a word that is never broken is better than a piece of delft.' This, however, is only the first lesson. One day, Papa comes across Sisty playing with his ivory domino set and asks him what he'd think if his mother threw the box out of the window 'for fun'.

> I looked beseechingly at my father, and made no answer.
>
> 'But, perhaps, you would be very glad,' he resumed, 'if, suddenly, one of those good fairies you read of could change the domino-box into a beautiful geranium, in a beautiful blue and white flower-pot, and that you could have all the pleasure of putting it on your mamma's windowsill?'
>
> 'Indeed, I would!' said I, half crying.
>
> 'My dear boy, I believe you; but good wishes don't mend bad actions; good actions mend bad actions.'
>
> So saying, he shut the door, and went out. I cannot tell you how puzzled I was to make out what my father meant by his aphorism; but I know that I played at dominoes no more that day.

All becomes clear the following day when his father suggests that they walk into town and that Sisty bring along his domino-box 'to show it to a person there'. On the way, they just happen to pass both a plant nursery and a china warehouse. The father inquires the prices – a fine double geranium costs 7s. 6.d and a pot 3s 6d. – but then says he has no money. Next they pop into a 'fancy stationers' and Papa casually asks how much the dominos are worth. Eighteen shillings is the answer; good to know, he replies, before walking out to leave Sisty alone in the shop. It will come as no surprise to learn that the dominos are sold, the plant and pot purchased, and that Mama, while delighted, wants to buy back 'your poor domino-box'. 'Shall we?' asks Papa, in the final test of the day. But Sisty has learned his lessons well:

Rebecca Coleman, 'Geranium & Sweet Pea Flower Children'. Watercolour and bodycolour on paper.

honesty; basic economics; the 'sanctity and happiness of self-sacrifice'; and most important of all, that 'I loved my father, and knew that he loved me'.[46]

If geraniums could occasionally teach little boys what it meant to be a man, they could also, and more often did, instruct little girls on

'Langage des Fleurs:
Geranium'. Bergeret
postcard, *c.* 1900.

how to be a woman. In George Eliot's *Middlemarch*, Sir James Chettan
is thought likely to prefer Celia to her sister Dorothea because 'Celia
is fonder of geraniums'.[47] But what did that fondness prove? It was
true that, as Harriet Beecher Stowe insisted, a woman would accrue
some physical and moral 'advantages' from 'stirring the soil and
sniffing the morning air', advantages including 'freshness and beauty
of cheek and brightness of eye, cheerfulness of temper, vigour of
mind, and purity of heart.'[48] But, more than that, Celia's association
with geraniums points to her 'more docile' nature, her willingness
to devote her time not to books or social reforms, but to a variety
of floral accomplishments whose quantity, if not quality, had only
increased since Mary Delany's time.

Rose-scented geranium signifying 'Preference', 1905, postcard.

Ivy geranium signifying 'Bridal Favours', 1905, postcard.

A fondness for geraniums might, for example, manifest itself in a desire to create a 'garland of green leaves and scarlet flowers' around a blancmange, or a decision to adorn a dress with some crocheted or knitted flowers, that would 'bear washing when soiled'; it might just mean pressing a leaf or two into a letter according to the latest version of the language of flowers.[49] After all, punned Leigh Hunt, 'one's flowers of speech' needed due care, 'to guard from blight as well as bathos.'[50] A rose geranium usually signified 'preference', nutmeg 'expected meeting' and lemon 'unexpected meeting'. The pencilled geranium meant 'ingenuity' and the silver-leaved 'recall', *P. triste* was self-explanatory, and an ivy-leaved geranium was either a bridal favour or a request to dance the next quadrille.[51] Nice girls could derive a 'constant fund of ecstasy' from their geraniumed correspondence.[52]

But what a liking for geraniums mostly told a man was that the woman in question had motherly potential. Victorian fiction and painting consistently associates pot-plant 'rearing' with the kind of practical and maternally inclined woman who can turn a house or a rented room into a home. In chapter Three, I mentioned the exemplary Peggotty from Dickens's *David Copperfield*, but even more poignant, for Dickens, is the prisoner's wife in *The Pickwick Papers*, who strives in the debtors' jail to take care of the 'wretched stump of a dried-up, withered plant', or brave Miss Tox in *Dombey and Son*, who, in the face of heartbreak, allows 'only one slip of geranium' to fall 'victim to imperfect nursing, before she was gardening at her green baskets, regularly every morning'.[53]

'Just like children' in their dependence on a 'keen, watchful, ever-attentive, thoughtful eye', geraniums were considered perfect companions for all manner of solitary women.[54] After the success of Thomas Hood's poem of 1843, 'The Song of the Shirt', the image of the sempstress in her lonely garret, yearning 'to breathe the breath / of the cowslip and primrose sweet', but making do with a spindly geranium, became a popular motif.[55] Although it was not particularly accurate, as most needlewomen worked in groups, Victorian culture found the combination of sickly girl and sickly plant compelling. Whereas Fanny Price and her geraniums had bloomed together, the Victorian plant/woman couple shared a life of martyrdom in the industrial city.

Governesses, invalids, orphans, widows and the lovelorn all sought comfort in a 'pet geranium' (as Amy in *Little Women* calls hers).[56] 'Pet' is an appropriate epithet for, if the plant was sometimes evoked as a kind of friend or sister – the motherless protagonist of *Jenny and Her Geranium* confides 'her thoughts and feelings' to her plant, which responds 'in an eloquent language all its own' – then its constant need for care was more like that of the cat which ideally accompanied it.[57] Rachel, in another story, thinks that 'her geranium was better to her than a doll' since 'if it were neglected it would die, if it was cherished it would live', while Revd Parkes recorded the gratitude of a widow to whom he had given a pot: 'I did not believe before that I should care for anything again in this world like I have cared for that geranium. Indeed, sir, I've almost got to love it as if it could speak.'[58]

'Is it possible, that a heart can so passionately love an inanimate object, cherish and coddle it like her own child?' So asks a Russian intellectual in an A. F. Veltman story of 1840 that may contain the 'first description of railroad travel in Russian literature'.[59] En route to St Petersburg, Alexander Fyodorovich observes a young peasant women who refuses to be parted from a 'huge flowerpot'. He inquires into their 'mysterious connection' and learns that the geranium had been a gift from a man she had once loved. When eventually the plant

Alice Squire, *Young Woman Reading (The Governess)*, 1861, watercolour.

turns out to have come from his despised rival, Minodora Pamfilovna abandons it without a second thought.[60]

Relationships with potted geraniums could last for years (which is why Minodora's is so big) and could even extend across generations (as well as Jenny's geranium, we meet its aged 'grandmother').[61] The contrast with bedding plants, which come and go in a single season and are therefore 'never old, never young', couldn't be greater. 'Look at a Scarlet Geranium,' instructed Forbes Watson, 'as you sometimes see it in a greenhouse, with its long woody stems continuing from year to year; it may be somewhat untidy but it can make you love it'.[62] And where one loves one also mourns, as the fervent opening of Charlotte S. M. Barnes's elegy bears out:

> Dry, sapless, withered, dost thou lie!
> No more thy buds will greet my eye –
> No more thy fragrance fill the air.
> Why art thou dead ? No watchful care
> Was spared to save thee; night and day
> I strove to shield thee from decay.
> But all in vain. Thy bloom is fled –
> Thy leaves have fallen – thou art dead![63]

Although elegies for geraniums weren't common, Victorian writers often provided evidence of emotional attachment by staging dramas of the loss, and happy return, of the plant or its pot. In *David Copperfield*, after Traddles loses his plant-stand and flower-pot (the beginnings of his 'house-keeping' and the only thing not 'plain and serviceable' that he'll ever own), Peggotty hurries off to Tottenham Court Road to reclaim it from the pawnbroker.[64] Jenny's geranium, meanwhile, is retrieved from the pub to which her father had taken it to barter for booze – 'just in time'.

But not all geraniums made it home again. Chapter Two of *Mary Barton*, Elizabeth Gaskell's 1848 'tale of Manchester life', features two lusty specimens on the broad window-sill of the Barton parlour, a room that's warm, cosy and 'almost crammed with furniture (sure sign of good times among the mills)'. As if to ward off envious glances, Mrs Barton keeps the curtains drawn while the geraniums, 'unpruned and leafy', form a 'further defence from outdoor pryers'. The scene is a cheerful gathering of family and friends, familiar from cottage genre painting, and it acts as a pivot in the novel. What came before was blissful – a day at Green Heys Fields, just a half an hour's walk away but a different world, 'thoroughly rural'. In particular, the farm-house garden whose 'scrambling and wild luxuriance' Gaskell details – 'roses, lavender, sage, balm . . . rosemary, pinks and wallflowers, onions and jessamine' – 'speaks of other times and other occupations'. Only two miles from Manchester, this is a vanishing place and its flowers are already fading into legend; 'there runs a tale that primroses may often be found.' Compared to the 'republican and indiscrimi-nate order' of the country garden, Mrs Barton's unpruned geraniums seem less impressive and ultimately they are unable to offer much 'defence' against the novel's relentless progress into the city slums. By the end of the third chapter, Mrs Barton is dead, and as scandal, des-titution and further deaths hit the family by insistently incremental degrees, the domestic haven that she had created is slowly disman-tled. In chapter Nine, we are told that in Manchester 'there are no flowers'. For Gaskell, no return to the British countryside was possi-ble and there was no place for its values in the industrial city. The only hopeful solution she could imagine was emigration. The novel closes with an image of Mrs Barton's daughter, Mary, in a cottage with a garden around it and 'far beyond that . . . an orchard'.[65] Mary is in Canada.

Sex, Death and Scarlet Geraniums

Over the course of the nineteenth century, as we've seen, most geraniums became angels in the house, but a few retained a little pre-Victorian sex appeal. Again the issue at stake was colour. In the lan-guage of flowers, 'scarlet geranium' could signify several different things. Charlotte Latour's enormously popular *Le Langage des Fleurs* (1819) established *sottise* as the first meaning, with a story of Madame de Staël's comparison of the flower with a tedious Swiss officer: 'it pleases the eye; but when you press it even lightly, it emits an unpleasant smell'.[66] In the book's many English editions, some translated *sottise* as 'stupidity' and others as 'folly' (which are not the same thing). Although later floral semioticians – in tune with public sentiment – reassessed the plant and declared it 'comforting', traces of those earlier associations often remained.[67] Robert Browning's geraniums, for example, always signal a kind of danger. In 'Pippa Passes', Ottima asks her lover to 'grope' his way through the window where 'tall / Naked geraniums straggle' in the 'blood-red' morning light, and in 'Evelyn Hope', when the narrator expresses grief at the death of a sixteen-year-old who had 'scarcely heard his name', he also confesses to being 'thrice as old' as the girl with lips of 'geranium's red'.[68]

A more socially acceptable geranium glow envelopes Bathsheba Everdene in Thomas Hardy's *Far from the Madding Crowd* (1874). We first see her as Gabriel Oak does, perched on a cart,

> surrounded by tables and chairs with their legs upwards, backed by an oak settle, and ornamented in front by pots of geraniums, myrtles, and cactuses, together with a caged canary – probably all from the windows of the house just vacated. There was also a cat in a willow basket, from the partly-opened lid of which she gazed with half-closed eyes, and affectionately surveyed the small birds around.

The cottage parlour has been broken into its parts, but the effect is another pictorial 'performance'. The 'whole concern' is framed by 'fresh, green' foliage and bathed in a 'scarlet glow' of sunshine which, in a 'leafless season', produced a 'peculiar, vernal charm': of which the crimson-jacketed Bathsheba, at its 'apex', is not unaware.[69] The complex 'drama of visual attitudes' that this scene introduces – Bathsheba blushes at the sight of herself blushing in a looking glass, the cat half-eyes the birds, and Gabriel Oak watches it all – will develop in the course of a novel whose romantic entanglements are consistently framed as a series of 'conflicting and competing' impressions.[70] Throughout them all, Bathsheba's glow continues to evoke a homely sex appeal.

The same cannot be said for Emma Bovary, the eponymous heroine of Gustave Flaubert's 1856 novel. Shortly after their marriage, Emma's husband Charles watches her leaning on the window-sill, 'between two pots of geraniums'. Charles is charmed, thinking perhaps, as Laurie Lee would do a hundred years later, 'such a morning it is when love / Leans through geranium windows'. But *Madame Bovary* is not *Cider with Rosie*. Charles may cast Emma in the role of contented comely housewife, but the reader can't help detecting an incipient sign of her yearning to escape. Even at this early stage of the story, Emma has already revealed herself as a much fussier specimen than a cottage geranium, and her idea of romance turns out to have many preconditions concerning the ideal lover's clothes, beard and location. 'Like some tropical plant, did love not require the correct soil and a special temperature?'[71] Charles and his geraniums are simply too provincial.

For Dostoevsky's characters, the problem with geraniums is not that they are dull but that they dazzle in a way that provokes much more than spring-cleaning. In *Crime and Punishment* (1866), Raskolnikov visits the apartment of the old woman he will later murder. He notices that 'there is not a speck of dust anywhere' and that the sun, shining though 'geraniums and muslin window-curtains', is 'bright'.[72] André Breton later chastised Dostoevsky for relaying such a series of 'clichés' and 'postcards' from a 'stock catalogue'.[73] But the stock catalogue is exactly the point: the unbearable cliché is precisely what stirs his nihilistic characters into action. In *The Devils* (1871–2), Stavrogin, a man from whom 'the Marquis de Sade could take lessons', confesses that he once raped a young girl whom he had found sitting sewing in front of her apartment window.[74] He remembers that 'there were lots of geraniums on the window-sill and the sun was shining very brightly'.

Three days later, the child, in 'despair', leaves the apartment to hang herself in a storeroom. Stavrogin knows what's happening but does nothing to stop her, transfixed instead by the sight of a tiny red spider on a geranium leaf. From then on, that image becomes a source of anguish for him, contaminating every dream of flowers and sunshine, every thought of happiness.[75] Geranium psychosis had arrived.

five

Brief Fall, then Inexorable Rise

꧁❀꧂

B y the end of the nineteenth century, a full repertoire of uses for geraniums had been established. This final chapter will chart the geranium's career through the twentieth- and into the twenty-first century, revisiting everything from bedding styles to pot-plant companionship to herbal medicine, and not forgetting, of course, the debate about redness.

The Problem with Geraniums

Geranium, houseleek, laid in oblong beds
On the trim grass. The daisies' leprous strain
Is fresh. Each night the daisies burst again,
Though every day the gardener crops their heads.
John Gray (1893)

I liked the pots of geraniums. I didn't much like the dust-bins. No, I did quite like the dustbins. In a way I liked the dustbins more than the geraniums. I thought the dustbins left more as it were scope for the imagination.
Michael Frayn (1977)[1]

At the end of chapter Three, I presented the case against bedding plants that was first mounted in the 1870s and – because the gerani-ums refused to go away – reiterated at regular intervals through to, and beyond, the First World War. As ever, the 'desperately aesthetic business' of gardening had a strong class dimension. If the presence of a geranium in your garden was usually deemed 'as damningly significant of crudeness and thoughtless of taste as a plush picture-frame on a parlor wall', that was largely because 'only the horticultural *bourgeoisie* allow geraniums to intrude among larkspur and foxgloves.'[2] Sometimes it seemed as if all that a satirist of the middle classes needed to do was mention a geranium and the work of exposing conventionality, pretension and 'stiffness' was done. Even Henry James took the shortcut. For Mrs Gereth in *The Spoils of Poynton* (1897), nothing is more suburban than 'iron pots, on pedestals painted white and containing ugly geraniums, ranged on the edge of a gravel path and doing their best to give it the air of a terrace.'[3]

Cover of *Spade Work: Or, How to Start a Flower Garden* by Henry Hoare (1902).

But if was unthinking to put a geranium in your flower bed and affected to place it on a terrace pedestal, it was beyond the pale to place it in the window. As the examples from the previous chapter suggest, the potted geranium sometimes seemed to have more in common with a piece of furniture than a plant, and nothing irritated modern sensibilities more than the overstuffed parlours of their Victorian forebears. 'How wonderful it would be if we could throw all the furniture out of the window', speculated Willa Cather in an essay that linked a cluttered drawing room with the detailed realistic style of nineteenth-century fiction.[4] It all had to go: the chintz, the doilies, the antimacassar and the china pot with its aspidistra or geranium. What a streamlined modern flat needed was an 'architectural', and even easier-to-ignore, cactus or rubber plant.[5]

Those who persisted with the pot in the window displayed, at best, a lack of imagination. In a 1919 short story called 'The "Heart's Desire"', where the title itself anxiously cordons off a cliché in scare quotes, H. M. Tomlinson describes a street in Millwall in which each grey house was identical except for 'its number and the ornament

Elizabeth M. Chettle, *Aston Hall, Birmingham*, 1906, watercolour.

which showed between the muslin curtains of its parlour windows. The home of the Jones's had a geranium, and so was different from one neighbour with a ship's model in alabaster, and from the other whose sign was a faded photograph askew in its frame.'[6] Suggesting distinction, these ornaments merely confirm sameness. In someone else's house, such signs helped to identify the occupant as not 'interesting' or lacking 'temperament', as a 1914 *Scribner's* reviewer put it; their presence in one's *own* house, however, could drive a young man to violence.[7] In Ronald Riching's short story 'The House of Blood' (1920), Garfield Lovell's disgust with tradition and 'bloodless' propriety finds its intense focus in the blood-red geraniums that have 'always flowered' in the window-boxes of the family home. 'How infuriatingly trim and stiff it all is,' he muttered, 'and how unnatural. Oh, you geraniums, why can't you nod in the breeze – or do something.'[8] But even nodding in the breeze isn't 'interesting' enough for Garfield; forced to 'do something', he brandishes a revolver at his aunt, and shoots himself in the chest.

Back in the garden, the advent of the First World War accelerated the trend towards the herbaceous or mixed border of perennials and shrubs. It was partly a question of labour shortages – 'I arranged it,' wrote Lady Alice Martineau, 'when war broke out that [the garden] need never be entered by any gardener, just a woman to weed and to mow the grass' – and partly of the cost and feasibility of heating a greenhouse for flowers rather than vegetables.[9] In 1917, in symbolic support for the campaign to make a U-boat-blockaded Britain self-sufficient in food, George V instructed that the geraniums surrounding Queen Victoria's monument at Buckingham Palace be dug up and replaced with cabbages and potatoes.[10] It was a gesture that had a lasting resonance, not least in *Mrs Dalloway*, Virginia Woolf's 1925 novel about the after-effects of the war on the lives of Londoners. For one of the novel's minor characters, Mr Brewer, managing clerk at the estate agents of Sibleys and Arrowsmiths, the war had only two significant consequences: it 'utterly ruined the cook's nerves' and it 'ploughed a hole in the geranium beds'. The latter phrase is striking

He can't grow much hair,
but he can grow
geraniums.

less for its predictable satire on suburban complacency – Mr Brewer has a 'waxed moustache' and lives in Muswell Hill – than for its force and inadvertent poignancy. Inspired by the same banal thoughts that led him to cultivate geraniums, Mr Brewer had urged one of his clerks, Septimus Warren Smith, to do his patriotic duty. In 1923, however, a shell-shocked Septimus can be found wandering aimlessly among the 'prim flowers' of Regent Park; the novel's climax is his horrific suicide by impalement on some iron railings. If pre-war London was full of geraniums, it was also full of 'young men called Smith' and, Woolf suggests, a hole has also been ploughed through a generation of greenhouse-tending clerks. But what's worse, the complacency of patriotism, and the foolishness of the lower middle classes, remains unshaken. Woolf describes a crowd of 'poor people' waiting outside Buckingham Palace for a glimpse of the Royal car: 'they waited; looked at the Palace itself with the flag flying; at Victoria, billowing on her mound, admired her shelves of running water, her geraniums.'[11] In 1922, the Greater London Fund for the Blind organized its first 'Geranium Day' collection. The flower had been chosen as a 'symbol of consolation'.[12]

It was to prove just as difficult to get rid of the geraniums as it was to let go of the old ideas about patriotism, empire and class, and by the radicalized Thirties, impatience with, and aggression towards, the symbols of passive contentment intensified. In 'Bagpipe Music' (1937), the poet Louis MacNeice attacked a populace whose aspirations were limited to a 'bit of a skirt in a taxi', a trip to the picture palace, 'a packet of fags when our hands are idle' and, of course, a 'country cot with a pot of pink geraniums', while in 'Autumn Journal' (1939), geranium, here in the form of scented bath soap, features as ones of the drugs of 'the present moment' that the narrator needs to resist if he is to become what he calls a 'man-in-action':

> I cannot lie in this bath for ever, clouding
> The cooling water with rose geranium soap.[13]

Clearly some drastic action was needed. In *Brave New World* (1932), Aldous Huxley had already imagined a bomb blast and 'a foot, with the boot still on it, flying through the air and landing, flop, in the middle of the geraniums – the scarlet ones; such a splendid show that summer!' In 'And the Seventh Dream is the Dream of Isis' (1933), David Gasgoyne was just as fleshy, and even more surreal:

> there is an explosion of geraniums in the ball-
> room of the hotel
> there is an extremely unpleasant odour of
> decaying meat
> arising from the unpetalled flower growing
> out of her ear[14]

Geranium Day, poster issued by the National Institute for the Blind.

While Victorian geraniums suffered so that little children could become good, modernist specimens suffered so that poets could make it new. T. S. Eliot's most famous geranium was dead and shaken by a 'madman' – a scenario that, he admitted, was adapted from Jules Laforgue's vision of 'diaphanous geraniums, warrior spells, / Monomaniac sacrileges!'[15] Laforgue's 'conceit', said Eliot, recalled the English Metaphysical Poets' method of 'transmuting ideas into sensations, of transforming an observation into a state of mind'. The modern poet had similarly to 'force, to dislocate if necessary, language into his meaning.'[16]

One idea that the young Eliot often addressed was that of the city, and mostly the 'sensation' into which he 'transmuted' it was stench. In 1917, the San Diego mayoral election styled the choice between industrial expansion and controlled 'city beautiful' planning as 'Smokestacks versus Geraniums', but for Eliot there was no opposition: geraniums *meant* smokestacks.[17] In 'Rhapsody on a Windy Night', the thought of 'sunless dry geraniums' recalls, and is recalled by, a heady concoction of chestnuts, cigarettes, 'cocktail smells', dust, eau de Cologne, and 'female smells in shuttered rooms'.[18] In another poem, 'Easter: Sensations of April', written in 1910 and unpublished in Eliot's lifetime, the geranium is presented in contrast with the daffodil. Part One features a 'little negro girl' returning from church with a red geranium for her 'third-floor window sill'. We seem to be in familiar Sunday School territory, the kind that lingered on in the cinema for decades. In the 'modern story' of D. W. Griffith's epic *Intolerance* (1916), the Dear One (Mae Marsh) discovers comfort in the city from her 'Hopeful Geranium'; in F. W. Murnau's *City Girl* (1930), Kate eventually swaps her pot plant and railroad apartment for Midwestern farm life; and in Jean Renoir's *La Grande Illusion* (1937) the prison camp commandant Von Rauffenstein finds solace in *la seule fleur de la fortresse*. No such luck for Eliot's 'little negro girl'. Despite her Christian care, the geraniums in her window become 'withered and dry'. The final stanza of the section 'repeats' the action of the first – the girl brings a geranium home – but the implication is that these 'little formulae of God' are

Still from *City Girl* (1930), directed by F. W. Murnau.

spiritually, as well as physically, inadequate. The quality that Eliot most associates with geraniums is odour, for 'their perfume comes / with the smell of heat / From the asphalt street'. Modern zonals are not noted for a particular scent but in the past, as Madame de Staël pointed out, their odour was considered 'unpleasant'. Some claimed they smelt of fish and Sylvia Plath suggested 'armpits' and a 'musky . . . lovebed'.[19] How different is the daffodil which Eliot describes in Part Two of his poem: resident in a 'cool secluded room', it smells, as an Easter flower should, 'of earth and rain'.[20]

Eliot's sense of the geranium as a waste land of a plant – modern, disgusting and desiccated – inspired a generation of writers to associate the flower with dirt, heat, anger, sweat, grease, pub sawdust, horseflies, dinginess and the gutter, or to imagine it in its pot, squashed like a flat-dweller in his 'too tight' apartment or abandoned in an alley, 'with its roots in the air'.[21] Since then, the destruction of geraniums has continued to give pleasure to writers opposed to some aspect of modern life or with a surrealist bent. In recent years, for example, the

Still from *Intolerance* (1916), directed by D. W. Griffith.

Still from *La Grande Illusion* (1937), directed by Jean Renoir.

songwriter Regina Spektor has staged a fight between 'alien geraniums', while in *Music for Torching* (1999), the novelist A. M. Homes subjects some suburban specimens to trampling, beheading and even fire: 'The flowers, not believing they are dead, hold their color, as though holding their breath.' The prize for anthropomorphizing a geranium must, however, go to William Kotzwinkle. In his novelization of *E.T.*, Kotzwinkle puts the extra-terrestrial in a closet with a pot plant. Just one 'pleading glance', soft murmur and gentle stroke from the 'space-botanist', and the plant bursts into bloom. '"Your voice is purest gro-formula, Ancient Master," said the geranium.'[22]

Redemption through Art

Unlike writers, painters never lost faith with geraniums. How could they when the near-at-hand plant pot offered so much? For some, it was the form of the zonal geranium – the contortions of its jointed stems and the distinctive shape of its leaves – that most intrigued. For others, it was the combination of plant and pot. We might compare Renoir's opulent Chinese tub in *Geraniums and Cats* (1881) with the self-effacing clay pot depicted by Cézanne in *Pot of Geraniums* (1885). Cézanne minimizes any distraction from the flat green solidity of the zonal leaves. More complicated patterns, involving similar leaves, can be found in Matisse's *Pot of Geraniums* (1912), although here their shape and colour (at the painting's focal point) are presented in a complex conversation with the plant's mossy pot and a series of other regularly spaced pots and staging shelves.[23] Juan Gris' Cubist *Pot of Geraniums* (1915) is even more intricate. A pyramidal still-life of pink and blue commercial patterns (wallpaper, fabric, newsprint) culminates in the organic design of the geranium's evenly spaced vibrant green leaves, poised between inside and outside, culture and nature. Geraniums have played a part in many different art movements – languishing droopily in Charles Rennie Mackintosh's Art Nouveau drawing of 1904, reduced to a series of overlapping geometric shapes in Lyubov Popova's Constructivist sketch of 1922, and replaced by black acrylic hand-lettering in John Baldessari's Conceptualist *Semi-close-up of Girl by Geranium* (1966–8).[24] Mostly, however, the geranium's supposed horticultural liability – its scarlet flowers – became its prime painterly asset.

The geranium's aesthetic rehabilitation began with the Impressionists, for whom a scarlet glow expressed the sunny comforts of middle-class life rather than its tedious conventionality. While the British art market demanded romanticized cottage scenes and poor

Pierre-Auguste Renoir, *Geraniums and Cats*, 1881, oil on canvas.

Paul Cézanne, *Pot of Geraniums*, c. 1885, pencil and watercolour on paper.

girls in attics, the Impressionists turned their attention to the leisured life of parks and family gardens.[25] The difference in perspective becomes clear if we compare the 'city girl' tradition with works like Mary Cassatt's *Young Woman Sewing in the Garden* (1880–82) and Childe Hassam's *Geraniums* (1888).[26] While the Victorian sempstress and her solitary

Henri Matisse, *Pot of Geraniums*, 1912, oil on linen.

pot plant sat in the dark trying to make a living, the the well-to-do Impressionist young woman, dressed virginally in white, sews for amusement surrounded by a profusion of red blossoms whose sun-lit bloom reflects, and decoratively frames, her own. These women don't need to make friends with their flowers; they rise above them (literally, in these compositions).

'Give me an apple tree in a suburban garden', said Renoir, 'I haven't the slightest need of Niagara Falls.'[27] The family garden

143

provided Impressionists with both a setting for the enactment of
the social and psychological theatre of 'modern life' and a *plein-air*
laboratory in which to conduct experiments on the changing effects
of light on colour. One of those colours was a vivid geranium red and
its presence, often in conjunction with its 'complementary' green,
can be detected in numerous paintings. Sometimes, as in Manet's

Charles Rennie Mackintosh, *Ivy Geranium, St Mary's, Scilly*, 1904, pencil and watercolour
on paper.

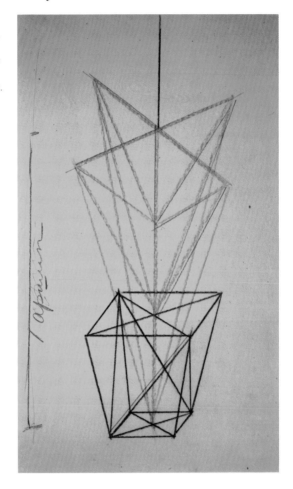

Lyubov Popova, 'Geranium in a Pot', prop design for the play *The Magnanimous Cuckold* by Fernand Crommelynck, 1922.

Liseuse (1879–80), geraniums simply allow the introduction of tiny vivid flecks of red – 'like spice!' said Derek Jarman – sometimes, they take centre stage.[28]

Claude Monet lived in, and painted, several gardens: beginning with his parents' home at Sainte-Adresse in Normandy and ending at Giverny which, although famous for its informal profusion, also featured two beds of red geraniums in the front of the apple-green house.[29] The garden that I want to consider here, though, is that of the Maison Aubrey in Argenteuil, a prosperous suburb eleven kilometres from Paris. Monet moved there in 1871 and soon established

Mary Cassatt, *Young Woman in the Garden*, c. 1880–82, oil on canvas.

a garden according to modern horticultural fashion, right down to the circular mounded beds of red geraniums set in the lawn.

Those beds feature in a number of paintings, the most intriguing of which is *Camille Monet on a Garden Bench* (1873). The painting is carefully divided in half by a dramatic diagonal separating sun and shadow. In the foreground shaded perhaps by a tree, sits a woman

Childe Hassam, *Geraniums*, 1888–9, oil on canvas.

on a black slatted bench. Dressed opulently in grey and black – the colours of mourning – she looks out of the canvas, while an elegant man in grey and black stands behind her, leaning on the bench. Both have touches of white at their collar and cuffs. Other visual echoes connect the pair – his left hand dangles over the edge of the bench, while hers, holding what might be a letter or a visiting card, is awkwardly raised – and their postures combine to form another diagonal that intersects with the first. While critics all agree that the effect of this composition is to cordon off the couple, various scenarios, including a tryst and a quarrel, have been offered to explain why. The most convincing interpretation, however, draws on biographical details to suggest this is a work about life and death. *Camille Monet on a Garden Bench* was the first of three garden paintings which Monet painted after the death of his father-in-law in 1873; all feature his wife and, from different angles, the geraniums.[30] Mary Gedo suggests that they might be 'components of a sequential narrative' about mourning and, with this in mind, critics have interpreted the bearded man either as a personification of Death, whose visiting card – and proffered bouquet – Camille is reluctant to receive, or, less allegorically, as 'Monet's alter ego' expressing his 'helpless inability to penetrate his wife's grief'.[31] But what of the other half of the painting? Gedo thinks that the woman near the geraniums 'might best be understood as an allusion to Camille's mother, the other person most affected' by the death, but doesn't say anything about the contrast

Claude Monet, *Mme Camille Monet on a Garden Bench*, 1873, oil on canvas.

Photograph of Monet's garden at Giverny.

the painting makes between its two parts.[32] A distinction is clearly made between shade and sun, between black and luminous red, between the mourning clothes of the couple at the bench and the standing woman's blue dress, and between a foreground dominated by geometrical lines and a background of organically rounded shapes: the woman's hat, her parasol, the flower bed and even the trunks of the trees are curved. The only comparable shape in the foreground is the bouquet on the bench whose fleck of red provides an understated link between the two parts of the painting. By reaching out to touch the sunlit geraniums, the woman with the parasol is connecting with life: might Camille, someday, do the same?

Sunshine and Sex

A red geranium was blooming there in the pot
when a butterfly madly came fluttering by
and who knows what she said –
the geranium blushed even more red –
that seductress butterfly.
(from 'The Seagull', sung by
Aliki Vougliouklaki in *Aliki in the Navy*, 1961)[33]

At stake for Monet was not the *language* but the *feeling* of flowers. Impressionism, said Pissarro, was 'based on sensations', a formulation that also applies to much of the art that followed in its wake.[34] One possible source of reinvigorating sensation involved contact with 'primitive' cultures or, at the very least, what Ruskin had shudderingly called 'primitive colours'.

In an essay of 1917 on the absurdity of snobbish and standardized aspirations, D. H. Lawrence imagined a petunia 'leaning over to a geranium and saying: '"Ah miss, *wouldn't* you just love to be in mauve and white, like me, instead of that common turkey red."' It was, he thought, a ridiculous question: people, and plants, should 'learn to do as they like'. After all, 'a petunia is a petunia, and a geranium is a geranium'.[35] It's probably safe to say that, for all his asserted even-handedness, Lawrence liked geraniums better than petunias. His writings contain numerous appreciations of the 'redness of the red geranium', which for him could never be 'anything but a sensual experience.' 'Imagine', he said, 'that any mind ever *thought* a red geranium!'[36] The sun-loving flower – whether an 'intense' red or 'joyously' pink – was not a social artefact or a symbol, but an expression of sexual nature at its most undiluted, forceful and, as his contemporary the poet Amy Lowell concurred, 'raw'.[37]

That rawness was not readily available in northern Europe. In *The Rainbow*, for example, Ursula thinks of the schoolroom, with its 'frowsy geraniums against the pale glass', as a kind of 'prison'.[38] Moreover, the little red that did exist in England was associated with unsexy turkeys or bedded-out bourgeois reproach. Katherine Mansfield, Lawrence's friend and fellow interloper into polite society, often felt inimidated by city geraniums. 'Why should they ask me every time I go near: "And what are you doing in a London garden?" They burn with arrogance and pride.'[39] If life was to be 'hot with colour' and 'gayer than a geranium in a pot', one first had to find the sun – in the Mediterranean, in Australia, in California. 'Here is the garden, with red geraniums,' Lawrence declares in another poem, 'it is warm, it is warm.'[40]

Mario Borgoni, Poster for Ente Nazionale Italiano per il Turismo, c. 1915.

British astonishment at sunshine was nothing new – Leigh Hunt, visiting Genoa in 1823, had announced that 'you learn for the first time in this climate what colours really are'[41] – but its increasing availability was a startling modern phenomenon. The interwar years saw the first stirrings of mass seaside tourism. In Italy, coastal towns competed for custom with posters featuring blue skies, blue sea and

GORLESTON-ON-SEA

**Official Guide and Accommodation Register (1/- Postal Order)
from Information Bureau, Room 7, Gorleston-on-Sea, Norfolk**

Train services and fares from (BRITISH RAILWAYS) stations offices and agencies

Poster advertising holidays in Gorleston-on-Sea, Norfolk, 1950.

NO
PARKING
WORRIES

Write Here
↓

HEAVEN <u>CITY</u> HOTEL
Year Round Service - Dinning Room - BAR

**WORLD'S TALLEST GERANIUM
IN DINING ROOM**

MUKWONAGO, WIS.   HIWAY 15   PHONE 16

Postcard advertising the 'world's tallest geranium in dining room', at Heaven City
Hotel, Mukwonago, Wisconsin.

often, in the foreground, a scarlet geranium. Trying to recreate the
mood of summer leases and Spanish lovers, British Rail adapted the
image for the Norfolk resort of Gorleston-on-Sea.[42] Other places –
far from the sea – had to lure customers with 'the world's tallest
geranium in dining room'.

Painting with Plants

Since the early twentieth century, gardeners have often claimed that
what they are doing is 'painting with living flowers', inspired perhaps
by Monet's garden at Giverny, which he himself declared his 'most
beautiful work of art', or by Gertrude Jekyll's garden at Munstead
Wood in Surrey.[43]

Reclaiming the flower beds from the 'alien' hands of the Victorian
head gardener was the first step in the Arts and Crafts campaign
against the 'ugly and false in art'.[44] The problem with the professional
gardener was that he liked a 'routine' requiring 'no imagination' and
'limited understanding'. He was a 'decorative artist' who turned out
gardens like 'coloured advertisements'. His version of gardening was
laborious but 'cheap of mental effort'. The role of the 'artist-gardener',

on the other hand, required little but mental effort. 'Hardly the placing of a single plant can be deputed to any other hand than his own,' wrote Jekyll, 'for though, when it is done, it looks quite simple and easy, he must paint his own picture himself – no one can paint it for him.'[45] Painting, in other words, was *placing* – Jekyll's four gardeners did the planting.[46]

Gertrude Jekyll had been a frequent contributor to William Robinson's weekly magazine *The Garden,* and she contributed a chapter on colour to his influential book *The English Flower Garden* (1883). Like Robinson, she often described gardening as 'painting a picture' but, unlike him, she did not see the need to give up entirely on formality and strong colour.[47] Used correctly (and that was the haughty mantra), no plant nor colour needed to be excluded from the gardener's palette, not even the geranium. 'Not once but many times', Jekyll noted, visitors had 'expressed unbounded surprise' to find bedding plants in her garden. '"I should have thought that you would have despised geraniums." On the contrary, I love geraniums.'

It was hardly the plant's fault if it had been 'grievously misused': 'a geranium was a geranium long before it was a bedding plant'. Jekyll often featured salmon shades in Italian terracotta pots, 'traditional from the Middle Ages, and probably from an even more remote antiquity' and, more surprising to her visitors, planted scarlet zonals en masse.[48]

But as there were geraniums and geraniums, there was 'bedding and bedding'. Mass planting was 'wrong' in unchanging geometrical blocks – placed 'monotonously or stupidly so as merely to fill the space' – and 'right' when done 'with a feeling for "drawing" or proportion'; that is, in long narrow drifts within a 'mixed border' of annuals, perennials and shrubs, whose 'picture' gradually evolved through the season.[49] Colour was the key, and 'harmony rather than contrast' the intended effect.[50] Jekyll advocated a gradual progression through groups of related colours; at each stage, one group would 'saturate the eye' and prepare it for the next stage in the spectrum. The supreme example of this is the 'river of colour' she created in her own 200-foot long, fourteen-foot wide double borders. Since 'cool' colours create a sense of distance and 'warm' colours diminish it, the latter were placed furthest away. The centre of the border was red: groups of geraniums, salvias, cannas and dahlias set against a background of tall hollyhocks and a crimson-leaved vine.[51] While the 'colour is strong and gorgeous,' Jekyll insisted, 'as it is in good harmonies, it is never garish.' Her preferred geranium was therefore 'Paul Crampel' whose scarlet was 'pure' but 'not *cruel*'; 'raw' was not a compliment for Jekyll. The bed then progressed on either side through oranges, yellows, ending up at one end with greys, and the 'palest' yellows and pinks and, at the other, with grey, lilac and purple tones – shades which, by 'the law of complementary colour', would provide relief for eyes 'saturated' with 'rich colouring'.[52]

The Jekyll idiom came so profoundly to dominate twentieth-century styles of gardening – in 2011, for example, the gardens of Clare College in Cambridge featured a startling red border filled with salvias, monardas, dahlias and scarlet geraniums – that it's easy

Herbert Cowley, 'Red section of south border at Munstead Wood', *c.* 1912, autochrome.

Jekyll-inspired planting at Clare College, Cambridge, 2011.

to forget that not everyone immediately understood the subtleties of 'intelligent combination'. In 1913, for example, an American visitor to Munstead complained that she had never seen 'such frightful examples of red geranium bedding . . . even in Newport or Bar Harbor'.[53]

For keen gardeners like Monet and Jekyll, there was something wonderful about the fact that natural objects could form transient living pictures. For those who, by contrast, believed that nature 'has had her day' and that modern life was best appreciated as an artful performance, the aesthetic appeal of red geraniums lay in their ability to 'look like fakes'.[54] Given its association with cosy domesticity, the geranium was a less obvious choice for Decadence than, say, the orchid, and yet looked at in the right way, even the most homely plant could be made to seem unnatural, strange and often grotesque. So Proust isolates the effect of sunlight on a red carpet as 'une carnation', or 'flesh-tint', of 'géranium' while Laforgue, in 'Pierrots', adapts the conventional image of geranium lips to describe a 'clownish mouth' which 'holds all enchanted, / Just like a singular geranium.'[55] Expressionist interest in the psychological effects of colour led to startling images such Carson McCullers's November sky, 'the colour of a winter geranium', against which her teenaged girls come and go talking of Michelangelo, and to Mersault's discovery, in Camus' *L'Étranger*, that the cemetery's red geraniums intensify the horror of the 'blood-red earth' falling on his mother's coffin. In Woolf's *To the Lighthouse*, Mr Ramsay finds that the 'urns with the trailing red geraniums' interfere with his attempts to follow a logical line of abstract thought from A to Z; Z 'glimmers red in the distance' but he's distracted by the red that's close at hand. The geraniums 'decorate' his 'processes of thought', and then come to embody them; increasingly, the plants' leaves seem like 'scraps of paper on which one scribbles notes'.[56]

But the intention was not always to disturb. Detailing the Berlin apartment building of his turn-of-the-century childhood, Walter Benjamin recalled the unusual effect of observing its courtyard from a train. From this point of view, 'the red geraniums that were peeping from their boxes accorded less well with the summer than the red feather mattresses that were hung over the windowsills each morning to air.'[57] The mattress is not valued as a substitute for the geranium (for nature) but in preference to it. Who needs plants

Geraniums in Montparnasse Cemetery, Paris, 2011.

when the city creates its own colour? And who needs geraniums when one can buy geranium-red lipsticks and nail-polishes? It's not make-up for those seeking the 'natural look'. In *Passing* (1929), Nella Larsen's Harlem Renaissance novel, Irene knows that her friend Clare is a fake, because her lips, 'painted a brilliant geranium-red', make her skin seem 'ivory'.[58]

Still in the Window

On 2 June 1964, the Chicago *Daily News* reported that four geraniums had been stolen from outside the home of a Mrs John Freeman. Why was this newsworthy? The article explained: 'Red geraniums are the symbol for open house in the South Shore area on 14 June. The open house will be a guided tour for both negroes and whites through selected homes in the area.' In June 1964, red geraniums were required to signal an absence of discrimination, something the thieves probably did not like; a month later, the Civil Rights Act outlawed racial segregation.

Reading the geranium in the window wasn't always so straightforward. On setting up Waverley House, one of Manhattan's first detention houses for prostitutes awaiting trial, Maude Miner decided to 'post no sign which would distinguish this from other red brick dwellings on the street'. She 'had not realized that it was marked until one of the girls returning to visit us said, "I knew where to find it all right. I just looked for the red geraniums."'[59] Miner was a probation officer, determined to save women from the 'slavery of prostitution', and determined to convert the red geranium from sex to respectability. It wasn't easy. In *To Kill a Mockingbird* (1960), Harper Lee's novel of Depression-era Alabama, a line of 'six chipped-enamel slop jars holding brilliant red geraniums' proves equally confusing. The 'tenderly cared for' plants are positioned along the fence of a 'dirty yard' filled with rusty farm implements, old shoes, an old dentist's chair, the remains of a Model-T Ford and much else. What do they advertise? Lawrentian sensuality? A desire to 'keep

'Geraniums 4 Are No More', photograph from the *Chicago Daily News* (2 June 1964).

clean' and be respectable?[60] If the townsfolk don't even know how to read Mayella Ewell's geraniums, how can they assess her claim to have been raped?

Sometimes geraniums have found themselves as unwitting shields for evil. They flourish in places they shouldn't. They advertise the respectability of homes that are anything but. An early example is 14 Fitzgeorge Street, a house whose 'unsullied brightness' acts as a reproach to its dingy Bloomsbury neighbours in M. E. Braddon's 1867 sensation novel, *Birds of Prey*.

> There were flowers in the windows; gaudy scarlet geraniums, which seemed to enjoy an immunity from all the ills to which geraniums are subject, so impossible was it to discover a faded leaf amongst their greenness, or the presence of blight amidst their wealth of blossom. . . . The freshly-varnished

street-door bore a brass-plate, on which to look was to be dazzled; and the effect produced by this combination of white door-step, scarlet geranium, green blind, and brass-plate was obtrusively brilliant.

But all is not what it seems in Fitzgeorge Street. The house's new tenant Philip Sheldon is a dentist, specializing in false teeth. Not content to advertise with a brass-plate, he attaches to his house, a 'neat little glass-case, on the level of the eye of the passing pedestrian' containing, in a grotesque echo of the white doorstep and scarlet geraniums, 'glistening white teeth and impossibly red gums'.[61] No. 14, despite itself, succeeds in expressing its tenant's (murderous) personality.

Other geraniums provided more effective cover. During the 1930s, Eglfing-Haar, a psychiatric unit near Munich, set up a 'special department' in which to 'euthanase' disabled children. The killing took place in a room that was bare except for a small white-tiled table and a geranium in the window. As Frederick Wertham noted, there was a something horrible about the care taken with a pot plant in a place in which babies and children were poisoned and their brains placed into carefully labelled jars.[62] Walker Percy's novel *The Thanatos Syndrome* revisits the incident, as it emerges in the 'confession' of an American priest, Father Smith, who had once visited the hospital and seen the 'beautiful plant, luxuriant, full of bloom'. Like Stavrogin in Dostoevsky's *The Devils*, Father Smith cannot escape geranium-induced hallucinations. For him, however, the plant's presence 'replays' synaesthetically as a smell – a combination of something 'sweet' and 'chemical'; 'the geranium with a trace of the Zyklon B'.[63] And Egling-Haar was not the only place in which homely touches mingled with murder. When the SS officer Kurt Gerstein first saw the gas chamber at Bełżec, he initially mistook it for a house because the building was surrounded by 'large pots of geraniums or other flowers'. Above the door, however, was the inscription 'Heckenholt Foundation', a reference, Gerstein later learned, to the name of the officer in charge of the diesel engine whose exhaust gases would

National Can's new Geranium Design

STEPS UP SALES APPEAL

To make a good line better, to make a best-seller into a real volume-smasher, National Can has introduced a new matched line of kitchenware brilliantly lithographed with an attractive geranium design. The flowers are bright red with leaves in natural, contrasting green set against a background of clear white.

This new, consumer-tested design adds modern beauty to such National Can standbys as:
BREAD BOXES (in two styles—oblong and two-compartment).
STEP-ON CANS (Sturdy — 10 qt. capacity).
CANISTERS (Matched set of four: — 1 lb. tea; 2 lbs. coffee; 5 lbs. sugar; 5 lbs. flour).
WASTE BASKETS (Choice of round 26-quart basket and oval 12½ quart basket).
DUST PANS (Hooded — improved steel edge).
MATCH SAFES (Sturdy, attractive).

For prices and further information on the new geranium decorated line, please write Dept. CA-1. **HOUSEWARES DIVISION**

NATIONAL CAN
C O R P O R A T I O N
110 East 42nd Street, New York 17, N. Y.

be used to kill the building's occupants. The whole process took 32 minutes.[64]

Stories of these atrocities, of the violation not only of human life but of domestic sanctuary, emerged during the 1950s, at a time when attention was particularly centred on the meanings and values of the home. The rapid postwar expansion of suburban housing and increased home-based consumerism led to a revival of the traditional image of:

> Geraniums in the winder
> Hydrangeas on the lawn
> And breakfast in the kitchen
> In the timid pink of dawn.

American advertisement for Armstrong Plaid Kitchen, 1954.

And it wasn't just Rodgers and Hammerstein who extolled the virtues of pot plants.[65] Geraniums featured prominently in 1950s TV shows and advertisements which presented the family kitchen as the iconographic centre not just of the house but of a prosperous new conservatism. In Ann Petry's novel *The Street* (1947), a young black domestic servant, sitting on a New York subway train, sees an ad for a 'miracle of a kitchen':

'Time for a Breather!' A 1956 advertisement for beer.

The advertisement she was looking at pictured a girl with incredible blond hair. The girl leaned close to a dark-haired smiling man in a navy uniform. They were standing in front of a kitchen sink – a sink whose white porcelain surface gleamed under the train lights. The taps looked like silver. The linoleum floor of the kitchen was a crisp black-and-white pattern that pointed to the sparkle of the room.

Casement windows. Red geraniums in yellow pots. . . .
Completely different from the kitchen of the 116th Street
flat she had moved into just two weeks ago. But almost
exactly like the one she had worked in in Connecticut.[66]

The family of the advertisement was largely a fantasy. More women
than ever had jobs outside the home and one of 1952's bestsellers was
The Can-opener Cookbook.[67]

The Market in Geraniums

Uneffected by wartime food shortages, Americans had grown geraniums consistently through the first half of the twentieth century. In
Britain, though, the 1950s saw a distinct revival of interest in the plants
that were now 'so old-fashioned that they appear ultra-modern'.
That was Eleanor Sinclair Rohde's view after visiting the Chelsea
Flower Show in 1949 and coming upon a display mounted by W.A.R.
Clifton, the 'only specialist grower' who had persisted between the
wars. 'No other flowers light up with such remarkable brilliance in
artificial light', said Rohde; surely geraniums would 'once more
become a cult'.[68] In 1950, a leader in *The Times* approvingly noted that
Kew Gardens was 'trumpeting defiance at the anti-geranium ranks'
by showcasing 'many shades and varieties of leaf' in an 80-yard display, and in 1952, in preparation for Queen Elizabeth's coronation,
20,000 specimens of the new favourite double zonal, 'Gustav Emich',
were planted in the Royal Parks, while lampposts along the proces-
sional route were festooned with hanging baskets filled with trailing
varieties.[69] The message was clear: the new Elizabethan Age was to be
filled with geraniums.

New books were published to reintroduce the plants, the first
being the American Helen Van Pelt Wilson's confusingly titled *Geraniums: Pelargoniums for Gardens and Windows* (1946) – renamed *The Joy of
Geraniums*, it was reprinted three times by 1965. In Britain a BBC TV
producer called John Cross wrote *The Book of the Geranium* (1951),

which included instructions on how to give suburban gardens 'an Italianate air' and a plea to interested readers to get in touch if they were interested in following the American example and forming a British Geranium Society.[70] They were, and since then, 'Geranium and Pelargonium' societies (there is no end in sight to the argument about the name) continue to flourish. While many of the traditional (fancy-leafed, rosebud, single- and double-zonal) varieties remain popular, new exhibition categories have also been added and, even today, many breakthroughs in hybridizing emerge from the greenhouses of amateur enthusiasts.

One of the great postwar proselytisers was Derek Clifford, whose books include *Pelagoniums, Including the Popular 'Geranium'* (1958). One variety that Clifford discussed were the Langley-Smith hybrids, developed in the 1920s, which he renamed Angels. Developed from crosses between Regals and the lemon-scented, crinkly-leaved *P. crispum*, the Victorian 'finger bowl geranium', Angels are distinguished by their delicate pansy-like flowers and have steadily grown in popularity.[71] Most other major introductions during last sixty years have been zonal hybrids. These range from the large bushy, floriforous 'Irenes' (introduced in Ohio in 1942 by Charles Behringer and named for his wife) to the small 'Deacons' (hybridized with ivy-leaved geraniums from the late 1960s by the Revd Stanley Stringer in Suffolk) and the 'oddities of the zonal family', the finger-flowered 'Stellars' and 'Formosums'. In the late 1950s Ted Both developed Stellars in Sydney by crossing zonals with a local cultivar called 'Chinese Cactus'; further hybrids have since been created by Ian Gillam in Vancouver.[72] Formosums, on the other hand, were only one of the many groups (others included dwarf and miniature zonals) that attracted the interest of the great Californian nurseryman, Holmes Miller. More recently, Cliff Blackman in Australia and Steve Pollard in Britain have experimented with 'Zonartics' – in which zonals are crossed with the 'snowy stork's bill' (*P. articulatum*) – to create plants with yellow flowers.[73] In 1823 Elizabeth Kent had predicted 'no end to the varieties of Geranium', but even she would have been surprised to learn that in 2011 over 16, 000 different cultivars existed.[74] In the greenhouses of enthusiasts and specialist nurseries, the experimentation shows no signs of ceasing.

Most of these plants, however, are not available to the casual garden centre shopper. The great majority of geraniums purchased today are commercially produced in one of two ways: by seed or by cutting. During the 1960s experiments into pelargonium seed propagation at Pennsylvania State University led to the development of FI varieties: that is, plants that are guaranteed to be true to type since the seed from which they are raised is produced each time by repeating the initial cross between the hybrid's two parents.[75] Seed-raised geraniums are particularly popular with growers, such as parks departments, who don't want to devote time and greenhouse space to cuttings and who need identical-looking plants for a single season only. Although the first commercially available variety, sold in 1967, was called 'Carefree', raising geraniums from seed has its drawbacks: young plants require a lot of heat early in the season and need to be chemically treated in

Pelargoniums for sale at Woottens Nursery, Wenhaston, Suffolk, 2010.

Alfred G. Froelich placing geranium cuttings in sand at Lincoln Park Conservatory, Chicago.

order to keep them the correct size and from shedding their petals. Moreover, only single-flowered forms are available.[76]

The geraniums sold in garden centres are produced by a small number of multinational companies from fresh cuttings derived from a closely guarded 'mother stock'. Syngenta, for example, roots and develops its cuttings in Kenya before sending them back to Holland and Germany to be packed in plug trays and pots and then distributed throughout Europe. Small nurseries buy cuttings as well as plug-plants from global firms so even when plants are locally grown the source tends to be the same. Although multinationals want plants that will do well in as many different climates as possible, they also have to adapt to local preferences. In Scandinavia and France, for example, trailing ('cascade') varieties are the most popular, while zonals are the first choice of the Germans and British. Deep red still accounts for at least 30 per cent of geraniums sold. Commercial breeders concentrate less on novelty than on traits of economic significance, such as resistance to disease and drought. The holy grail is the industrial micropropagation of a 'self-cleaning' plant – one whose petals will fall off naturally, obviating the need for dead-heading.[77]

In the United States, sales of annual bedding plants doubled between 1949 and 1959, and since then the market has continued to gather momentum, 'like a heavily loaded wheelbarrow being pushed downhill'.[78] Bedding plants constitute the largest part of horticultural sales, generating approximately $2 billion per annum in the U.S. alone. For every $6.38 Americans spent on herbaceous perennials in 2005, they paid another $17.15 for bedding plants. Put another way, roughly 120 million geraniums are grown annually, just in the U.S.; the industry benefits tremendously from the fact that few consumers treat their plants as tender perennials that can be overwintered with minimal care.[79] Many of these plants are found in homes and gardens but as the images in this book testify, geraniums accompany us everywhere

Pelargonium rust on underside of leaf.

Pelargonium plant grown from tissue culture.

– from the maternity hospital car-park to the shopping mall, with its 'pyramid-shaped planters filled with half-dead' specimens, to the grave.[80] In parks and other civic gardens, annual bedding has never really gone away, despite attempts to persuade gardeners to replace double zonals with more insect-friendly flowers. 'But no other flower is so good tempered' and reliably floriferous.[81]

Victorian styles also linger in children's fiction, much of which has remained faithful to the cautionary-tale mode in which a plant's need of nurturing can test a boy or girl. In the 1920s, while the modernists were blowing holes in geranium beds, Cicely Mary Barker was reinventing Pre-Raphaelite kitsch in her 'Flower Fairy' books,

Cicely Mary Barker,
'The Geranium Fairy',
from *Flower Fairies of the Garden* (London, 1944).

The GERANIUM Fairy

one of the most popular twentieth-century children's series. The first was published in 1923 and 'The Geranium Fairy' appeared in 1944's *Flower Fairies of the Garden*, a wartime celebration of 'red, red, vermillion red / with buds and blooms in a glorious head!'

> Her name – Geranium – ev'ryone knows;
> She's just as happy wherever she grows,
> In an earthen pot or a garden bed –
> Red, red, vermilion red![82]

In recent years, stories of the cheerful adaptability of the geranium have been offered to help children and adults come to terms with modern variations on traditional scenarios. A grandparent's move to a nursing home can be eased by making sure 'Granny and

Pam Smy, Cover
of Linda Newbery,
Lob (Oxford, 2010).

her geranium were back together'; a daughter's absence from her sick
mother is sidestepped with the gift of a pot to 'be your company all
summer . . . just imagine that it's me'.[83] Today when urban children
express their rural longings by wishing 'we had a garden', their parents respond 'we just can't afford it, in London. And we have to be
in London for our jobs.'[84] In the end, it seems, everyone is content
to settle for pot-plant consolation. As the bestselling Evangelical
self-help writer Barbara Johnson puts it, it's 'hard to stick a perky
geranium in your hat and be gloomy!'[85]

Good Smells and Bad Coughs

Much of this book has been about the strong impression made by
brightly coloured flowers. In this final section, I'd like to revisit some
other parts of the pelargonium plant that have also, if less obtrusively, made an impact: its leaves and roots. I'll begin with scented-
leaved varieties – whose popularity in Victorian homes I touched on

in chapter Four – and end by updating the herbal medicine story that began in the seventeenth century.

'Do you remember smelling the geraniums in the late afternoon in the hall?' Katherine Mansfield wrote to her cousin in 1922. 'It seemed just the time and the place to smell those geraniums – I can't even imagine what going back there would be like; it would be too great a happiness. But I shall remember that day forever.'[86] Because its effects are often so transient, scent produces the most precise of sensual associations and the slightest whiff can awaken a long-suppressed memory. The scent of geranium leaves can resemble everything from lemon to camphor, but it's the 'pungent spray of rose-geranium' that most often revives 'a breath of the old life'. 'So it is', notes the narrator of a Turgenev story, 'that the faint fragrance from an unimportant flower outlives all the joys and miseries of a man – and eventually outlives the man himself.'[87]

Perhaps the most famous sensual remembrance in modern fiction is that experienced by Marcel in Proust's *À la recherche du temps perdu*, after he dips his *petit madeleine* into his tea. Before he hit on this formula, however, Proust experimented with other combinations in an earlier work, *Contre Sainte-Beuve*. He describes coming home on a snowy evening and trying to warm up with some dry toast and tea, 'a thing I never drink':

> I dipped the toast in the cup of tea and as soon as I put it in my mouth and felt its softened texture, all flavoured with tea, against my palate, something came over me – the smell of geraniums and orange-blossom, a sensation of extraordinary radiance and happiness.[88]

In a single moment, winter has given way to summer, and taste has given way to smell. The substitution of one sense by another, synaesthesia, is a common feature of Proust's work, and geraniums are often involved. Elsewhere Marcel hears a piece of music that evokes colour, taste and 'all the perfumed silkiness of a geranium'.[89]

Here, however, the ordinariness of the geranium, not to mention that of the tea and toast, contributes to the joy and radiance its scent provokes.

Many descriptions of scented geraniums are similarly pleasant but occasionally the pungent leaves lead to unwanted revelations. In his narrative of life as a slave in Cuba, Juan Francisco Manzano describes what happened when, while walking one day in the garden with his mistress, he casually picked and ripped apart a 'small leaf from a geranium'. Back in the confines of the house, his mistress immediately detected the fragrance: 'She grabbed my hands, smelled them, and picked up the pieces, which became a pile, a bush, an outstanding audacity.'[90] How dare he steal her scent? So she breaks his nose.

It didn't take long before the pungent smell was put to commercial use. In 1819, a chemist in Lyon discovered that the oil extracted from the glandular hairs of some scented-leaved geranium cultivars had similar chemical constituents (geraniol, linalool and citronellol) to that obtained from rose petals. Geraniums were much cheaper to grow and harvest, and in 1844 the first geranium plantations were established near the perfume town of Grasse in Provence. Production soon shifted to the French colonies of Algeria and Morocco and, after 1880, the island of Réunion (then called Bourbon). Today geranium-oil is mostly produced in China, followed by Egypt, Algeria and Morocco, with plantations also thriving in Australia, India and South Africa.[91]

Harvesting by hand takes place two or three times a year just as the plant comes into flower. The leaves and stems are picked in the morning and left to dry for a day before being subjected to steam distillation. The plants used are mostly descended from crosses between *P. capitatum* and usually *P. graveolens* or *P. radens*, and the chemical composition (and price) of the oil varies according to the cultivar used and the growing conditions.[92] In 1999, the price per kilo ranged from $160 for Chinese '*P. graveolens* oil' to $360 for 'Geranium Rose Maroc'.[93] Geranium oil is used in the manufacture of both single-note

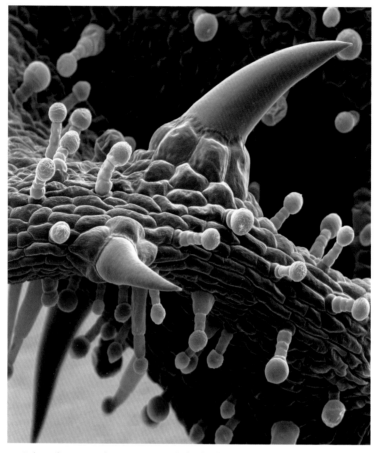

Coloured scanning electron micrograph (SEM) of gland hairs on leaf of pelargonium.

perfumes such as Lanvin's 'Géranium d'Espagne' (1925) – reputedly a favourite of Joan Crawford – and Frederic Malle's 'Géranium Pour Monsieur' (2009), and complex largely synthetic blends, such as Rochas's 'Moustache' (1948) and 'Paris' by Yves Saint Laurent (1983). While no fragrance has anything to do with the zonal geranium, its easily identifiable image often appears on the packaging of products containing geranium oil.

Perfumery represents only a small part of the fragrance market. Approximately 220 tons of geranium oil (with annual value of nearly £7 million) is sold annually for use in the production of all manner

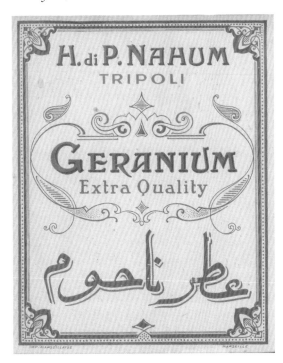

Geranium oil label from Libya.

of soaps, creams, detergents and air-fresheners, as well as in the aroma-therapy industry.[94] It is also used as a flavouring and preservative in drinks, ice-cream, baked goods, jams and chocolate. On a smaller scale, domestic cooks add scented leafs to cakes and jams, to contribute a citrus, rose or peppermint flavour.[95] As is the case in horticulture, only a few species of *Pelargonium* have yet been commercially exploited and research is currently taking place into a variety of species and cultivars which have shown 'potential as odourants for the perfumery and food industry, antimicrobial agents and insecticides'.[96]

The herbal medicine industry has also developed apace since the London apothecaries first encountered the 'sad geranium' (*P. triste*) in 1632. In recent years, most attention has focused on *Pelargonium sidoides*, an elegant species whose 'frilly grey leaves and dark magenta blooms' have become popular with gardeners looking for a 'rather subtle' container plant.[97] Known as umckaloabo in Xhosa click lan-guage, the roots of *P. sidoides* have traditionally been used in southern

Geranium oil label from Nigeria.

African folk medicine for the treatment of respiratory conditions. Umckaloabo first attracted European interest in the early twentieth century when Charles Stevens, a young entrepreneur from Birmingham, claimed that the herbal remedy had cured his tuberculosis. 'Consumption cures' were ten-a-penny until the advent of antibiotics in the 1950s, but Stevens is still remembered because of the drastic action he took to defend his reputation against charges of quackery by the British Medical Association and because he may have been a model for the purveyor of 'Tono Bungay' ('Ton o' Bunk, Eh?') in H. G. Wells's 1909 novel.[98] Stevens sued the BMA twice, without success, and then continued to sell his product, whose exact composition he refused to disclose. Two years before he died, D. H. Lawrence was given some by his sister. 'I duly take the Umbckaloaba

Distillation of geranium. Photograph from *L' Industrie des Parfums à Grasse*, c. 1900.

Geranium leaf used to flavour crab-apple jelly.

Liquid extraction of *P. sidoides* by the company True Botanica.

capsules,' he wrote to her, 'and can't see they have any effect on me whatsoever.'[99] Today compounds containing *P. sidoides* are marketed throughout Europe for the relief of symptoms associated with a variety of respiratory tract conditions, from the common cold and sinusitis to bronchitis. In Germany, where Schwabe Pharmaceuticals have trademarked the name Umckaloabo, sales amounted to $55 million in 2002.[100] A recent Cochrane Systematic Review examined the clinical evidence and reported that the preparations 'may be effective' but that 'doubt exists'.[101]

Postscript

You can't imagine the Holy Ghost sniffing at cherry-
                 pie heliotrope.
Or the Most High, during the coal age, cudgelling
                his mighty brains
even if he had any brains: straining his mighty mind
To think, among the moss and mud of lizards and
                  mastodons
To think out, in the abstract, when all was twilit
              green and muddy:
'Now there shall be tum-tiddly-um, and tum-
                tiddly-um,
hey-presto! scarlet geranium!'
We know it couldn't be done.
    D. H. Lawrence, 'Red Geranium and Godly Mignonette'

The Dormouse lay there, and he gazed at the view
Of geraniums (red) and delphiniums (blue),
And he knew there was nothing he wanted instead
Of delphiniums (blue) and geraniums (red).
    A. A. Milne, 'The Dormouse and the Doctor'[1]

I end this book with the story of two sick people who nurtured, and exulted in, their scarlet geraniums. If this sounds like another Victorian morality tale, in some ways, I suppose, it is. But the moral

Angelo Morbelli, *Vasi di Gerani*, 1919, oil on wood.

isn't clear, perhaps because one writer was thinking of a broad expanse of bedding plants and the other of a pot geranium.

The filmmaker and artist Derek Jarman spent the last year of his life gardening at his cottage in Dungeness and writing *Chroma*, an autobiographical meditation on white, red, blue and yellow. The section on the 'nature of red' begins with his recollection of an encounter, at the age of four, with a bed of geraniums in the courtyard of a villa on the banks of Lake Maggiore. 'This red had no boundary, was not contained. These red flowers stretched to the horizon.' Over fifty years, red accrued many other associations for Jarman – his mother's nail varnish, his father's face on seeing that polish on his son's nails, socialism, traffic lights, rednecks, love and, most recently, the 'violent red soreness' of eczema, the light of an eye test to determine how fast his sight was fading, and the virulent cells of the AIDS virus – but, through it all, the benchmark remained *Pelargonium* 'Paul Crampel'. If the 'scarlet of flower beds' was 'civic, municipal, public red', it was also a very personal red, 'the colour of flaming June' and of childhood. Each autumn while taking cuttings, Jarman was able to 'see' his past at Lake Maggiore. 'Other colours change', he said; 'The grass is not the green of my youth. Nor the blue of the Italian sky. They are in flux. But the red is constant.'[2]

After Katherine Mansfield was diagnosed with tuberculosis in 1917, she began to travel widely in pursuit of a good climate and a cure. In May 1921 she settled in the Swiss village of Montana-sur-Sierre, setting up home in a balconied chalet high under the glaciers and surrounded by pine forests. She was lonely and wrote often to her friends, sometimes about the time she spent 'taking care' of her geraniums and observing the growth of their buds. 'An exciting thing happened today,' she confided in one letter, 'My ancient geranium which is called Sarah has been visited by the angel at last. This geranium has *real personality*. It is so fearfully proud of this new bud that every leaf is curling.'[3] But Mansfield did not only want a geranium companion. Like Jarman and Lawrence, she was drawn to the luminous red of its flowers. In another letter, she described her balcony:

It is as big as a small room, the sides enclosed and big double doors lead from it to my workroom. Three superb geraniums still stand on the ledge when it is fine, and their rosy masses of flower against *blue space* are wonderful.[4]

After reading this letter, I came across a painting that seems to illustrate the scene perfectly. The Milanese Pontillist Angelo Morbelli completed *Vasi di Gerani* in 1919, just two years before Mansfield arrived in Switzerland, and, as far as I'm aware, she never saw it.[5] The blue expanse of mountains and sky is what Morbelli's canvas mostly represents, yet the space is broken by the delicate architecture of the balcony and a modest grouping of terracotta pots. The effect is not just one of scale but of colour. The sublime may be there in the distance but, near at hand and slightly off-centre, the potted geraniums have their own glow.

Timeline

18 million years ago	DNA evidence dates the first pelargonium to around this time
10–2 million years ago	*Pelargonium* undergoes its greatest period of diversification, as different species emerge and disperse
c. first millenium AD	Khoisan and Bantu inhabitants of southern Africa begin to use pelargoniums medicinally
1621	The first record of a pelargonium is the inclusion of *P. triste* in René Morin's plant catalogue
1672	Paul Hermann collects the ancestor of 'Regals', *Pelargonium cucullatum*, from Table Mountain
1690	*Pelargonium zonale*, as ancestor of modern Zonals, is illustrated in the *Hortus Botanicus Amsterdans*
1700	The ivy-leaved pelargonium (*Pelargonium peltatum*) is sent from the Cape to Amsterdam
1714	*Pelargonium inquinans*, the other ancestor of modern Zonals, is recorded in the Fulham Palace garden
1732	Dillenius names the seven 'African geraniums' in the *Hortus Elthamensis* 'pelargoniums'
1753	Linnaeus's *Species Plantarum* does not recognize the genus *Pelargonium* as distinct from *Geranium*

1772	Francis Masson becomes the first dedicated plant collector employed by Kew Gardens; his bounty includes 102 species of *Pelargonium*
1782–1792	Charles-Louis L'Héritier establishes the distinction between the genera of the Geraniaceae family
1820–1830	Robert Sweet's five-volume work, *Geraniaceae*, published
1844	The first plantations of 'rose geranium' established in Provence launch the 'geranium oil' industry
1859	In *On the Origin of Species* Charles Darwin notes the 'complicated' crosses achieved with *Pelargonium*
1967	The first commercially available FI seed variety is sold
1977–1988	A twenty-year review of genus *Pelargonium* results in the three-volume *Pelargoniums of Southern Africa*
2006	The chloroplast genome of a variety of *P. x hortorum* is published
2011	*International Register and Checklist of Pelargonium Cultivars* lists over 16,000 varieties

References

Introduction

1 Bosley Crowther, '*Honeymoon*', *New York Times* (19 May 1947).
2 'I Love Geraniums', music by Leigh Harline and lyrics by Mort Greene. Despite singing (or, rather, being dubbed singing) about her love for geraniums, Temple does not yet have one named for her. She has had to make do with a double-flowered white peony.
3 Wallace Stevens, 'Notes on a Supreme Fiction', in *Collected Poetry and Prose* (New York, 1997), p. 338.
4 'The Point of View', *Scribner's Magazine*, LVI/I (1914), pp. 130–31.
5 Ed Dorn, 'Geranium', *The Newly Fallen* (New York, 1961), p. 4.
6 'Dove's Foot' (also a reference to the five elongated seedheads) was another common name. *Culpeper's English Physician and Complete Herbal* (London, 1653), p. 72.
7 Quoted in William J. Webb, *The Pelargonium Family* (London, 1984), p. 6. The Greek for crane is *geranós* and for stork, *pelargós*. *Erodium*, a third member of the Geraniceae family, is named for the heron (*erodiós*). The family also contains *Monsonia* ('optionally' including *Sarcocaulon*) and *Hypsechocharis*. As Alastair Culham has recently written, 'the delimitation of Geraniaceae has varied, and its relationships remain uncertain.' 'Geraniaceae', in V. H. Heywood, R. K. Brummit, A. Culham, A. and O. Seberg, *The Flowering Plants of the World* (London, 2007), p. 255.
8 Carl Linneaus, *Species Plantarum: A Facsimile of the First Edition, 1753*, vol. II (London, 1959), pp. 676–83.
9 Forty-four uncoloured plates were published as 'Geraniologia' in 1792. Part of the manuscript is held in the Conservatoire Botanique in Geneva.
10 Another confusion exists in southern Africa where the plants came to be known, in Afrikaans, as 'malva', which 'gives the impression that the plant is a member of the Malvaceae and not the Geraniaceae' family. J.J.A. van der Walt and Ellaphie Ward-Hilhorst, *Pelargoniums of Southern Africa* (Cape Town, 1977), p. ix.
11 Henry C. Andrews, *Geraniums* (London, 1805–6), Introduction. Other catalogues of the period distinguish 'Geranium' from 'Geranium.

Pelargonium'. See, for example, Dickinson and Co.'s *Catalogue of Hot-house, Green-house, Hardy, and Herbaceous Plants: Flowering and Evergreen Shrubs, Fruit and Forest Trees* (Edinburgh, 1794).

12 M. H. Abrams, *The Mirror and the Lamp* (Oxford, 1953), p. 312.

13 William Wordsworth, 'A Poet's Epigraph', in *The Major Works* (Oxford, 2000), p. 151; Ralph Waldo Emerson, 'Blight', in *The New Oxford Book of American Verse*, ed. Richard Ellmann (Oxford, 1976), p. 77.

14 John Ruskin, Preface to Second Edition of *Modern Painters*, vol. I (London, 1857), p. xxxiii.

15 Leigh Hunt, 'A Flower for Your Window', *Leigh Hunt's London Journal* (17 September 1835), p. 193.

16 Derek Jarman, *Modern Nature* (London, 1991), p. 11.

17 Christopher Lloyd, *The Adventurous Gardener* (London, 2011), p. 121.

18 Diana Miller, *Pelargoniums* (London, 1996), p. 23; Hazel Key, *Pelargoniums* (London, 1993), p. 5.

19 See, for example, Derek Lee, 'Pelargonium or Geranium', *Pelargonium and Geranium News*, 5 (Spring 2010), pp. 25–7 and, in response, Diane O'Brien, 'Pelargonium or Geranium', *Pelargonium and Geranium News*, 7 (Autumn 2010), p. 7.

1 Out of Africa

1 Frédéric-Emmanuel Demarne, '"Rose-scented Geranium": A *Pelargonium* Grown for the Perfume Industry', in *Geranium and Pelargonium*, ed. Maria Lis-Balchin (London, 2002), p. 194.

2 Cynthia S. Jones et al., 'Leaf Shape Evolution in the South African Genus Pelargonium L' Hér. (Geraniaceae)', *Evolution*, LXIII/2 (2009), pp. 479–97.

3 Recent research (by Manning, Goldblatt, Struck, Van der Walt and Bakker) is summarized in Omar Fiz et al., 'Phylogeny and Historical Biogeography of Geraniacae in Relation to Climate Changes and Pollination Ecology', *Systematic Botany*, XXXIII/2 (2008), pp. 326–42.

4 Peter Goldblatt and John C. Manning, 'Plant Diversity of the Cape Region of Southern Africa', *Annals of the Missouri Botanical Gardens*, 89 (2002), p. 293.

5 Ibid., pp. 297–8.

6 Marianne North, *Abundant Beauty: The Adventurous Travels of Marianne North, Botanical Artist* (Vancouver, 2010), pp. 195–6.

7 Charles Darwin, *The Annotated Origin: A Facsimile of the First Edition of On the Origin of Species* (Cambridge, MA, 2009), p. 490. Darwin himself briefly visited the Cape in 1836.

8 Goldblatt and Manning, 'Plant Diversity of the Cape Region', pp. 295, 283.

9 John Manning, *Field Guide to Fynbos* (Cape Town, 2007), p. 15.

10 Ibid., p. 14.

11 Custodians of Rare and Endangered Wildflowers (CREW) Programme, at www.sanbi.org, last accessed 28 May 2012; *The Red List of South African*

Plants 2011, at http://redlist.sanbi.org, last accessed 28 May 2012.

12 New South Wales Endangered Species Listing, at www.environment.nsw.gov.au, last accessed 28 May 2012; The IUCN Red List of Threatened Species, at www.iucnredlist.org, last accessed 28 May 2012.

13 Manning, *Field Guide to Fynbos*, p. 22. See also F. T. Bakker et al., 'Nested radiation in Cape Pelargonium', in *Plant Species-level Systematics*, ed. Bakker et al. (Rugell, 2005); G. A. Verboom et al., 'Origin and Diversification of the Greater Cape Flora', *Molecular Phylogenetics and Evolution*, 51 (2009), pp. 44–53; Jan Schnitzler et al., 'Causes of Plant Diversification in the Cape Biodiversity Hotspot of South Africa', *Systematic Biology*, 60 (2011), pp. 1–15; Ben H. Walker et al., 'Consistent Phenological Shifts in the Making of a Biodiversity Hotspot: The Cape Flora', BMC *Evolutionary Biology* (2011), p. 39.

14 F. T. Bakker et al. 'Phylogenetic relationships within *Pelargonium* sec. *Pesistera* (*Geraniaceae*) inferred from nrDNA and cpDNA sequence comparisons', *Plant Systematics and Evolution*, 211 (1998), pp. 273–87.

15 Omar Fiz et al., 'Phylogeny and Historical Biogeography of Geraniacae', p. 326 (Abstract).

16 Diana Miller, 'The Taxonomy of *Pelargonium* Species and Cultivars, their Origins and Growth in the Wild', in *Geranium and Pelargonium*, ed. Lis-Balchin, p. 65.

17 Mike Fraser and Liz Fraser, *The Smallest Kingdom: Plants and Plant Collectors at the Cape of Good Hope* (London, 2011), p. 20.

18 Thomas Johnson, *The Herball or Generall Historie of Plantes* (London, 1633), p. 948.

19 Arthur Macgregor, *Tradescant's Rarities* (Oxford, 1983), p. 20.

20 Prudence Leith-Ross, 'A Seventeenth-century Paris Garden', *Garden History*, XXI/2 (Winter 1993), p. 156.

21 John Parkinson, *Theatrum Botanicum* (London, 1640), p. 709.

22 Jacques-Phillipe Cornut, *Canadensium plantarum* (Paris, 1635), ch. 44. The plant is also included in 'Elysium Britannicum' by John Evelyn (another Morin customer) and in the catalogue produced by William Lucas's plant shop in the Strand in 1677. John Evelyn, *Elysium Britannicum, or The Royal Gardens*, ed. John E. Ingram (Philadelphia, 2001), p. 109; John Harvey, *Early Gardening Catalogues* (London, 1972), p. 23.

23 Fraser and Fraser, *The Smallest Kingdom*, p. 167. For an account of a *P. triste* tuber, 10 cm in diameter and 35 cm in length, see Webb, *The Pelargonium Family*, p. 9.

24 Culpeper, *English Physician and Complete Herbal*, p. 73.

25 Parkinson, *Theatrum Botanicum*, p. 709.

26 J.J.A. van der Walt, with illustrations by Ellaphie Ward-Hilhorst, *Pelargoniums of Southern Africa* (Cape Town, 1977), vol. I, pp. 3, 5, 12, 20, 23, 26, 33, 40, 46. Manning, *Field Guide to Fynbos*, p. 182.

27 James Petiver, 'Some Farther Account of Diverse Rare Plants', *Philosophical Transactions*, vol. XXVII (1710–11), p. 420.

28 Ray Desmond, *Kew: A History of the Royal Botanic Gardens* (London, 1995), p. 91.

29 By 1710, a further ten species had been added. Diana Miller, *Pelargoniums* (London, 1996), p. 16.

30 David Jacques and Arend Jan van der Horst, *The Gardens of William and Mary* (London, 1988), p. 169.

31 Before he became commissioner of the Hortus, Huydecoper tried to restrict the supply of botanical material from the Cape; afterwards, he wanted as much as possible. Harold Cook, *Matters of Exchange: Commerce, Medicine and Science in the Dutch Golden Age* (New Haven, CT, 2007), p. 321.

32 Wilfrid Blunt and William T. Stearn, *The Art of Botanical Illustration* (London, 1994), p. 153.

33 D. O. Wijnands, *The Botany of the Commelins* (Rotterdam, 1983), p. 108.

34 Anne Wilkinson, *The Passion for Pelargoniums* (Stroud, 2007), p. 24.

35 Jacques and van der Horst, *The Gardens of William and Mary*, p. 179.

36 Desmond, *Kew*, p. 107.

37 Sue Minter, *The Apothecaries' Garden* (Stroud, 2008), p. 12.

38 Sandra Morris, 'Legacy of a Bishop (Part 2): The Flowers of Fulham Palace Gardens Introduced, 1675–1713', *Garden History*, XXI/1 (Summer 1994), p. 18; Alice M. Coats, 'The Hon. and Revd Henry Compton, Lord Bishop of London', *Garden History*, IV/3 (Autumn 1976), p. 19.

39 Molly McClain, *Beaufort: The Duke and his Duchess, 1657–1715* (New Haven, CT, 2001), p. 211.

40 Jacques and van der Horst, *The Gardens of William and Mary*, p. 173.

41 Douglas Chambers, '"Storys of Plants": The Assembling of Mary Capel Somerset's Botanical Collection at Badminton', *Journal of the History of Collections*, IX/1 (1997), p. 51.

42 Ibid., p. 47.

43 Jenny Uglow, *A Little History of British Gardening* (London, 2004), p. 109.

44 McClain, *Beaufort*, pp. 210–11.

45 Ibid., pp. 212–13; Minter, *The Apothecaries' Garden*, p. 12.

46 James Petiver, 'An Account of Divers Rare Plants', *Philosophical Transactions*, vol. XXVII (1710–11), p. 392.

47 John Aubrey, *Aubrey's Natural History of Wiltshire*, ed. John Britton (Newton Abbott, 1969), p. 93. His source was 'Mr Watts, gardener of the Apothecary's garden at Chelsey, and other botanists'.

48 Petiver, 'Some Farther Account', pp. 420–21.

49 Tim Fulford, Debbie Lee and Peter J. Kitson, *Literature, Science and Exploration in the Romantic Era* (Cambridge, 2004), p. 91.

50 Quoted in Frank R. Bradlow, 'Introduction' to *Francis Masson's Account of Three Journeys at the Cape of Good Hope, 1772–1775* (Cape Town, 1994). p. 63.

51 *Francis Masson's Account*, p. 111.

52 Mia C. Karstan, 'Masson's Journeys at the Cape', *Journal of South African Botany*, XXIV/4 (October 1958), p. 185.

53 *Francis Masson's Account*, p. 135.

54 Miller, *Pelargoniums*, p. 18; Bradlow, Introduction to *Francis Masson's Account*, p. 53; Fraser and Fraser, *The Smallest Kingdom*, pp. 87, 90.

55 Mary Gribbin and John Gribben, *Flower Hunters* (Oxford, 2008),

pp. 124–5.

56 Bradlow, Introduction to *Francis Masson's Account*, p. 63.

57 Fraser and Fraser, *The Smallest Kingdom*, p. 120.

58 Desmond, *Kew*, p. 107.

59 Quoted in Christopher Irmscher, *The Poetics of Natural History* (New Brunswick, NJ, 1999), p. 13.

60 Ibid., p. 25. On British geraniums in India, see Eugenia Herbert, *Flora's Empire* (Philadelphia, 2011).

61 Barbara Wells Sarudy, *Gardens and Gardening in the Chesapeake, 1700–1805* (Baltimore, MD, 1998), pp. 18, 163.

62 Ann Leighton, *American Gardens in the Eighteenth Century* (Boston, MA, 1976), p. 283.

63 Grant Thorburn, *Forty Years' Residence in America* (Boston, MA, 1834), p. 74. Lydia Maria Child, *Letters from New York* (New York, 1843), p. 53. Thorburn was the model for Lawrie Todd in John Galt's novel of 1830 of the same name.

64 William Cobbett, *The American Gardener* (London, 1821), no. 349.

65 See www.calflora.org and Ken Owen, 'An Island Called Santa Cruz: Removing Invasives on the Channel Islands', *Cal-IPC News*, XII/2 (Summer 2004), p. 5. Alan Weisman describes 'feral geraniums' in Northern Cyprus. *The World Without Us* (New York, 2007), p. 97.

2 New Familiars

1 Bengt Jonsell, 'Linnaeus, Solander and the Birth of Global Plant Taxonomy', *Enlightening the British*, ed. R.G.W. Anderson et al. (London, 2003), pp. 92–3.

2 Lisbet Koerner, *Linnaeus* (Cambridge, MA, 1999), pp. 39–40.

3 Ann B. Shteir, 'Gender and "Modern" Botany in Victorian England', *OSIRIS*, 2nd series, 12 (1997), p. 29.

4 Wilfrid Blunt and William T. Stearn, *The Art of Botanical Illustration* (London, 1994), p. 326.

5 Gill Saunders, *Picturing Plants* (Berkeley, CA, 1995), p. 96.

6 First cultivated at Chelsea in 1724, the plant was known as 'Geranium africanum arborescens, malvae florio'. William T. Aiton, *Hortus Kewensis*, 2nd edn (London, 1812), vol. IV, pp. 174–5.

7 Paul Hulton and Lawrence Smith, *Flowers in Art from East and West* (London, 1979), p. 13. See also Mark Laird, 'The Congenial Climate of Coffeehouse Horticulture', in *The Art of Natural History*, ed. Therese O'Malley and Amy R. W. Meyers (Washington, DC, 2008), pp. 231–4. Each plate was dedicated to a subscriber to the series; in this case, to the botanist William Sherard.

8 The second volume contains paintings by Daniel Frankcom, an under-footman at Badminton trained by Kickius. Gloria Cottesloe and Doris Hunt, *The Duchess of Beaufort's Flowers* (Exeter, 1983), pp. 9–10; Molly McClain, *Beaufort: The Duke and his Duchess, 1657–1715* (New Haven, CT,

2001), pp. 213–14; Blunt and Stearn, *The Art of Botanical Illustration*, p. 146.

9 Saunders, *Picturing Plants*, p. 48.

10 Mark Laird, 'The Culture of Horticulture: Class, Consumption and Gender in the English Landscape Garden', in *Bourgeois and Aristocratic Cultural Encounters in Garden Art, 1550–1850*, ed. Michael Conan (Washington, DC, 2002), p. 242. See also John Harvey, *Early Gardening Catalogues* (London, 1972), pp. 176–82.

11 Laird, 'The Congenial Climate of Coffeehouse Horticulture', p. 234.

12 Saunders, *Picturing Plants*, p. 104.

13 *Inquians* also featured in the January selection. Other pelargoniums were available in July, September and October.

14 Alicia Wiesberg-Roberts, 'Introduction (I) Mrs Delany from Source to Subject', in *Mrs Delany and her Circle*, ed. Mark Laird and Alicia Weisberg-Roberts (New Haven, CT, 2009), p. 9.

15 Delany, quoted in Ruth Hayden, *Mrs Delany: her Life and Her Flowers* (London, 1980), pp. 112, 131.

16 Blunt and Stearn, *The Art of Botanical Illustration*, p. 174.

17 Erasmus Darwin, *The Botanic Garden, Part II: Containing the Loves of the Plants, a Poem* (Lichfield, 1789), vol. II, p. 61.

18 Maria Zytaruk, 'Mary Delany: Epistolary Utterances, Cabinet Spaces and Natural History', in *Mrs Delany and her Circle*, p. 134.

19 Lisa Ford, 'A Progress in Plants: Mrs Delany's Botanical Sources', in *Mrs Delany and her Circle*, pp. 216–220.

20 David Elliston Allen, *The Naturalist in Britain* (Princeton, NJ, 1976), p. 38.

21 Mark Laird, 'Mrs Delany's Circle of Cutting and Embroidery in Home and Garden', in *Mrs Delany and Her Circle*, p. 163.

22 Harvey, *Early Gardening Catalogues*, pp. 56, III.

23 Laird, 'Mrs Delany's Circle', p. 166.

24 Mary Russell Mitford, *Our Village* (London, 1832), vol. V, p. 129.

25 Saunders, *Picturing Plants*, p. III.

26 See Wiesberg-Roberts, 'Introduction (I)', p. 7, figure II.

27 The plants on the lid of the Derby soup tureen are given as 'cordifolio geranium' (that is, *P. cordifolium*, named for its heart-shaped leaves) and 'terebinthinum geranium' (*P. graveolens*). On Edwards, see Saunders, *Picturing Plants*, pp. 55–8.

28 Amanda Vickery, *Behind Closed Doors: At Home in Georgian England* (New Haven, CT, 2009), p. 176.

29 Samantha George, *Botany, Sexuality and Women's Writing, 1760–1830* (Manchester, 2007), ch. 2.

30 Jean-Jacques Rousseau, quoted in Amy M. King, *Bloom: The Botanical Vernacular in the English Novel* (Oxford, 2003), p. 50.

31 Janet Browne, 'Botany for Gentlemen: Erasmus Darwin and *The Loves of the Plants*', *Isis*, LXXX/4 (December 1989), p. 597.

32 Richard Polwhele, *The Unsex'd Females* (1798), note to l. 33, in *Revolutions in Romantic Literature*, ed. Paul Keen (Toronto, 2004), p. 269. Polwhele's primary target is Mary Wollstonecraft.

33 The model was Rousseau's *Lettres élémentaires sur la botanique*, written to teach botany to the daughter of a friend. The book was translated into English by Thomas Martyn in 1785. See Shteir, 'Gender and "Modern" Botany', p. 35.

34 Priscilla Wakefield, *An Introduction to Botany, in a Series of Familiar Letters*, 5th edn (London, 1807), p. 120.

35 [Maria Elizabeth Jackson], *Botanical Dialogues, between Hortensia and her Four Children* (London, 1797), pp. 178–9.

36 Browne, 'Botany for Gentlemen', p. 614.

37 Ibid., pp. 600, 596. See also King, *Bloom*.

38 Frances Arabella Rowden, *A Poetical Introduction to the Study of Botany* (London, 1801), pp. 189–90.

39 Christine Battersby, *Gender and Genius* (London, 1989), p. 71.

40 William Cowper, *The Task*, Book 3, l. 578 (London, 1855), p. 113.

41 The line rhymed with 'most graceful too about the hips'. Robert Rabelais, *A Nineteenth Century, and Familiar History of the Lives, Loves, and Misfortunes, of Abeillard and Heloisa* (London, 1814), p. 76.

42 Bob Dylan, *Blonde on Blonde* (Columbia, 1966).

43 Thomas Erskine, *The Geranium* (London, 1795), pp. 1–4. The poem had previously circulated anonymously, or wrongly attributed, in anthologies of 'warm yet elegant poems' such as *The Festival of Love* (Dublin, 1789), *The Amorous Jester* (London, 1785) and *The Cabinet of Love* (London, 1792).

44 Polwhele, *The Unsex'd Females*, l. 29.

45 Thomas P. Slaughter, *The Natures of John and William Bartram* (New York, 1996), pp. 63–4.

46 Alexander Nemerov, *The Body of Raphaelle Peale* (Berkeley, CA, 2001), p. 18.

47 *Thomas Jefferson's Garden Book, 1776–1824*, ed. Edwin Morris Betts (Philadelphia, 1944), p. 383.

48 In November 1807, Jefferson wrote to his granddaughter Martha that he had 'struck some sprigs of geranium in a pot'. Ibid., p. 354.

49 Margaret Bayard Smith, *The First Forty Years of Washington Society*, ed. Gaillard Hunt (New York, 1906), p. 385.

50 *Thomas Jefferson's Garden Book*, pp. 382–3.

51 Carol Eaton Soltis, 'Rembrandt Peale's "Rubens Peale with a Geranium": A Possible Source in David Teniers the Younger', *American Art Journal*, XXXIII/1–2 (2002), pp. 12, 15.

52 Nemerov, *The Body of Raphaelle Peale*, pp. 18–19.

53 Ibid., p. 119. Copies of the 'Peale Pot' are sold by Guy Wolff pottery, at www.guywolff.com, last accessed 28 May 2012.

54 Charlotte Murray, *The British Garden* (1799), quoted in Elizabeth A. Dolan, *Seeing Suffering in Women's Literature of the Romantic Era* (Aldershot, 2008), p. 107.

55 Jean-Jacques Rousseau, *Reveries of the Solitary Walker*, trans. Russell Goulbourne (Oxford, 2011), p. 72.

56 Charlotte Smith, 'To the Goddess of Beauty', quoted in Dolan, *Seeing Suffering*, p. 115.

57 Charlotte Smith, *Minor Morals*, quoted in Dolan, *Seeing Suffering*, p. 109. Botany was often presented as an 'antidote to levity and idleness' but also to the dangers of 'pernicious habits'. Wakefield, *An Introduction to Botany*, p. v.

58 Cowper, *The Task*, Book 3, ll. 566–9, p. 112.

59 Charlotte Smith, *Conversations Introducing Poetry* (London, 1804), p. 117. Being from the southern hemisphere, species of pelargoniums flowered in the European winter.

60 Jane Austen, *Mansfield Park* (Harmondsworth, 1984), pp. 46, 173, 174.

61 Cowper, *The Task*, Book 3, l. 675, p. 117.

62 Judith W. Page and Elise L. Smith, *Women, Literature, and the Domesticated Landscape: England's Disciples of Flora, 1780–1870* (Cambridge, 2011), p. 221.

63 Smith, *Conversations Introducing Poetry*, p. 117.

64 Jane Loudon, whose praises of the east window I quote, suggests it as a setting for a few 'tall and spreading geraniums, with showy trusses of flowers' – but 'any more than five or six would give the window the appearance of being a substitute for a greenhouse, a most unpleasant idea at any time, and particularly so in the country.' *The Lady's Country Companion; or How to Enjoy a Country Life Rationally*, 2nd edn (London, 1846), pp. 18–19.

65 Austen, *Mansfield Park*, pp. 384, 421.

66 Ibid., p. 282.

67 Barbara Hardy, 'The Objects in *Mansfield Park*', in *Jane Austen: Bicentenary Essays*, ed. John Halperin (Cambridge, 1975), p. 184.

68 Emily Dickinson, *The Complete Poems* (London, 1986), p. 234; *The Letters of Emily Dickinson*, ed. Thomas H. Johnson (Cambridge, MA, 1958), p. 235.

3 Bedding and Breeding

1 [Sir James Edward Smith], 'Masson (Francis)', in *Encyclopaedia Londinensis*, vol. XIV (London, 1816), p. 515.

2 Jenny Uglow, *A Little History of British Gardening* (London, 2004), p. 198.

3 Robert Sweet, *Geraniaceae*, 5 vols (London, 1820–30), I, no. 4, 31, 81. These are all hybrids of *P. cucullatum*.

4 R. Todd Longstaffe-Gowan, 'James Cochran: Florist and Plant Contractor to Regency London', *Garden History*, XV/1 (Spring 1987), p. 61.

5 Sweet, *Geraniaceae*, vol. I, no. 92.

6 Ray Desmond, *A Celebration of Flowers: Two Hundred Years of Curtis's Botanical Magazine* (London, 1987), p. 61. The National Trust has recently re-established part of Colt Hoare's pelargonium collection at Stourhead.

7 William Cobbett, *The English Gardener* (Oxford, 1980), p. 240.

8 In 1824 de Candolle divided the genus into twelve sections; William Harvey's *Flora Capensis* (1860) increased this to fifteen, and a sixteenth section was recognized by Dreyer et al. in 1992. Dreyer et al., 'Subdivision of *Pelargonium* sect *Cortusina* (Geraniaceae)', *Plant Systematics and Evolution*, 183 (1992), pp. 83–97. See also Miller, 'The taxonomy of *Pelargonium* species and cultivars' (which updates her 1996 book *Pelargoniums*), and F. T. Bakker et al., 'Phylogeny of *Pelargonium* (Geraniaceae) Based on DNA

Sequences from Three Genomes', *Taxon*, 53 (2004), pp. 17–28.

9 One of the aims of the Geraniaceae Group is recreate Sweet's primary hybrids. at www.geraniaceae-group.org, last accessed 28 May 2012.

10 William Makepeace Thackeray, *Vanity Fair* (Oxford, 2008), p. 44.

11 Maggie Campbell-Culver, *The Origin of Plants* (London, 2001), p. 156.

12 Anne Wilkinson, *The Passion for Pelargoniums* (Stroud, 2007), p. 87.

13 As the book was alphabetically arranged, the image also features a pelecinid wasp. T.d.B, 'Pelargonion', in *Dictionnaire pittoresque d'histoire naturelle et des phénomènes de la nature*, ed. F. E. Guérin-Meneville (Paris, 1833–9), vol. VII, pp. 228–31. See also Sweet, *Geraniaceae*, vol. I, No. 32 and No. 83; Wilkinson, *The Passion for Pelargoniums*, p. 100.

14 Mary Woods and Arete Swartz Warren, *Glass Houses* (London, 1988), p. 91.

15 Humphry Repton, *The Landscape Gardening and Landscape Architecture of the Late Humphry Repton*, ed. J. C. Loudon (London, 1840), p. 217.

16 Mike Fraser and Liz Fraser, *The Smallest Kingdom: Plants and Plant Collectors at the Cape of Good Hope* (London, 2011) p. 117.

17 Cobbett, *The English Gardener*, p. 39; Repton, *The Landscape Gardening*, p. 217.

18 Thackeray, *Vanity Fair*, p. 532.

19 Leigh Hunt, *The Descent of Liberty: A Mask* (London, 1815), p. 28.

20 The conservatory intoxication scene culminates in the 'strange drugged dream' into which Madame Walter falls after exposure to 'the cloying fragrance of the weird tropical plants' in Guy de Maupassant's *Bel-Ami* (1885), trans. Douglas Parmée (Harmondsworth, 1974), p. 401.

21 George Eliot, *The Mill on the Floss* (Oxford, 2008), p. 441.

22 Ibid., pp. 442, 363, 521.

23 Charles Dickens, *David Copperfield* (Oxford, 2008), pp. 5, 20, 611.

24 Ibid., p. 385.

25 Ibid., pp. 281, 681, 846; Amy M. King, *Bloom: The Botanical Vernacular in the English Novel* (Oxford, 2003), p. 141.

26 J. C. Loudon, *The Green-house Companion* (London, 1824), Preface. Loudon himself had patented a curved wrought-iron glazing bar in 1816. The next big step was in the production of plate glass in the 1830s.

27 Ibid., p. 153.

28 Uglow, *A Little History*, p. 178.

29 Brent Elliott, *Victorian Gardens* (Portland, OR, 1986), p. 12.

30 George and Weedon Grossmith, *The Diary of a Nobody* [1892] (London, 1999), pp. 11, 22.

31 J. C. Loudon, *The Suburban Gardener and Villa Companion* (London, 1838), p. 9.

32 Ibid., pp. 356, 109–10.

33 Elliott, *Victorian Gardens*, pp. 13, 135.

34 Miriam Rothschild, *The Rothschild Gardens* (London, 1996), p. 132.

35 Loudon, *The Suburban Gardener*, p. 213, 229.

36 See Michael Waters, *The Garden in Victorian Literature* (Aldershot, 2008), ch. 1.

37 Repton, *The Landscape Gardening*, p. 365.

38 Loudon, *The Suburban Gardener*, p. 164.

39 Loudon, *The Green-house Companion*, p. 3.

40 H.R.C., *One Trial: A Novel* (London, 1860), vol. I, p. 278.

41 Uvedale Price, 'Essay on Architecture and Buildings', in *Essays on the Picturesque* (London, 1810), vol. II, p. 255.

42 Leigh Hunt, 'A Flower for Your Window', *Leigh Hunt's London Journal* (17 September 1835), p. 193.

43 'Cereus Traingularis', *The Florist's Journal* (1 January 1841), p. 1.

44 *Goethe's Theory of Colours*, trans. Charles Lock Eastlake (London, 1840), pp. 28, 323. Complementary colour theory was later 'given the force of law' in *De la loi du contraste simulatané des couleurs* (1838) by Michel-Eugène Chevruel, head of the dyeing department at the Royal Gobelins tapestry works in Paris. John Gage, *Colour in Art* (London, 2006), p. 49.

45 Hunt, 'A Flower for Your Window', p. 193.

46 Coventry Patmore, 'The Morning Call', in *The Angel in the House* (London, 1863), p. 56.

47 S. W. Patridge, *Our English Months* (London, 1862), p. 132.

48 Elizabeth Gaskell, *Wives and Daughters* [1866], (London, 1996), p. 15.

49 Elliott, *Victorian Gardens*, pp. 90, 146; Anne Wilkinson, *The Victorian Gardener* (Stroud, 2006), p. 151.

50 R. Fish, 'A Few Days in Ireland', *The Journal of Horticulture and Cottage Gardener* (10 March 1863), pp. 184–5.

51 Shirley Hibberd, *The Amateur's Flower Garden* (London, 1871), p. 17.

52 D. Thomson, 'The Panelling System of Planting Long Flower Borders', *The Journal of Horticulture and Cottage Gardener* (4 March 1862), p. 451.

53 Shirley Hibberd, 'A Geranium Pyramid', *The Floral World* (July 1864), p. 150. The pyramid also appears in the 1892 edition of Hibberd, *The Amateur's Flower Garden* (p. 82) and has recently been reconstructed at the Geffrye Museum in London.

54 'Notes on Pelargoniums', *The British Florist* (1 January 1841), p. 40.

55 Patmore, 'The Paragon', in *The Angel in the House*, p. 25.

56 Loudon, *The Green-house Companion*, p. 77; Mary Russell Mitford, *My Garden*, ed. Robyn Marsack (London, 1990), pp. 120, 122.

57 David Stuart, *The Plants That Shaped Our Gardens* (London, 2002), p. 74.

58 Edward Beck, 'The Pelargonium', *The Florist* (November 1848), p. 301.

59 Edward Beck, *A Treatise on the Culture of Pelargoniums* (London, 1846), p. 5.

60 J. Robson, 'A Bundle of Wants in the Bedding Geranium Way', *The Horticultural Journal and Cottage Gardener* (22 April, 1862), p. 65. See also Wilkinson, *The Passion for Pelargoniums*, pp. 124–3; Key, *1001 Pelargoniums*, p. 47.

61 Dr T. Foster, 'Calender of Flora and Fauna', *The London Medical Repository* (1 August 1819), p. 122. The name *P. hortorum* (and the name *P. domesticum* for Regals) was introduced by L. H. Bailey in *The Standard Cyclopedia of Horticulture* (New York, 1916), vol. V, pp. 253–3.

62 Hibberd, *The Amateur's Flower Garden*, p. 80; Donald Beaton, 'Development of Colour in Flowers', *Journal of Horticulture and Cottage Gardener*, 6 August 1861, p. 354. Beaton's ambition was to create geraniums with blue or yellow flowers. Shirley Hibberd, 'Geraniums', *The Horticulturalist* (July 1870), p .209.

63 Sweet, *Geraniaceae*, vol. III, no. 226.

64 A single-flowered zonal has five petals per floret; a semi-double, six to nine; a double, ten or more. See Peter Grieve, *A History of Variegated Zonal Pelargoniums* (London, 1868) and, for a fictional account of a florist who makes '£300 by "Mrs Pollock" alone', Thomas Miller, *My Father's Garden* (London, 1867), p. 138.

65 Frances Trollope, *Paris and the Parisians in 1835* (London, 1836), vol. II, p. 351.

66 Derek Jarman, *Modern Nature* (London, 1991), p. II.

67 *The Floral Magazine*, vol. VII (1868), following plate 377.

68 Shirley Hibberd, 'Bedders and Bedding in 1864', *The Floral World* (July 1864), p. 196.

69 Hibberd, 'A Geranium Pyramid', p. 150.

70 Charles Darwin, *The Variation of Animals and Plants Under Domestication* (New York, 1887), vol. II, p. 201. See also, for example, Charles Darwin, 'Crossing Breeding in Plants', *Journal of Horticulture and Cottage Gardener* (28 May, 1861), p. 151.

71 Darwin, *The Annotated Origin*, p. 251.

72 Darwin, *The Variation of Animals and Plants*, vol. II, pp. 301, 263, 147.

73 Ibid., p. 33. He later experimented with crosses of 'common' and peloric pelargoniums 'to discover whether with changes in structure of flower there is any change in fertility of pollen or of female organs'. *The Correspondence of Charles Darwin*, vol. II (1863) (Cambridge, 1999), p. 60.

74 Henry Lonsdale, *John Dalton* (London, 1874), p. 101. The OED lists 'geranium-coloured' from 1836 and 'geranium' (as a colour) from 1842, but I've found numerous earlier examples.

75 John Ruskin, 'Light', in *Lectures on Art* (Oxford, 1875), p. 162.

76 Gordon N. Ray, *William Makepeace Thackeray* (London, 1955), vol. I. p. 286.

77 John Ruskin, 'The Roots of Honour', in *Unto This Last and Other Writings*, ed. Clive Wilmer (London, 1997), p. 171. Quiller-Coach cited Dickens's liking for scarlet geraniums as evidence of his lack of interest in rural life. *Charles Dickens and Other Victorians* (Cambridge, 1925), p. 64.

78 Mamie Dickens, 'Dickens and his Children', *New York Times* (17 March 1884).

79 Charles Dickens, *Martin Chuzzlewit* (Oxford, 1998), p. 622.

80 Charles Dickens, *Dombey and Son* (Oxford, 2001), p. 465.

81 Charles Dickens, *The Letters of Charles Dickens*, ed. Madeline House and Graeme Storey (London, 1965), vol. VIII, p. 643.

82 Mamie Dickens, *My Father as I Recall Him* (London, 1886), pp. 61, 63.

83 Peter Ackroyd, *Dickens* (London, 1990), p. xi.

84 Arthur Paterson and Helen Allingham, *The Homes of Tennyson* (London, 1905), note accompanying plate between pp. 64–5. Alfred Tennyson, 'Amphion', in *The Works of Alfred, Lord Tennyson* (Ware, Hertfordshire, 1994), p. 195. William Robinson quotes these lines in *The Wild Garden* (London, 1870), p. II.

85 Nathaniel Hawthorne, 'The Birth-mark', *Tales and Sketches* (New York, 1982), pp. 764–80.

86 John Ruskin, *The Poetry of Architecture* (London, 1893), p. 205.

87 Forbes Watson, *Flowers and Gardens* (London, 1872), p. 122.

88 Hibberd, *The Amateur's Flower Garden*, pp. 17, 5, 34.

89 Ruskin, *The Poetry of Architecture*, p. 156.

90 William Morris, 'Making the Best of It', in *Hopes and Fears for Art* (Bristol, 1994), p. 90.

91 Richard Ellmann, *Oscar Wilde* (London, 1987), p. 252.

92 Elliott, *Victorian Gardens*, pp. 148–9.

93 Robinson, *The Wild Garden*, p. 13.

94 Octavia Hill, 'Colour, Space and Music for the People', *The Nineteenth Century* (May 1884), 741–52.

95 Thomas Hardy, *Tess of the D'Urbervilles* (London, 1998), p. 38. Ruskin too thought that the 'very bright red' brick used in contemporary housing was 'one of the ugliest colours that art ever stumbled upon' and 'destructive of natural beauty'. *The Poetry of Architecture*, pp. 189–90.

96 Nathan Cole, *The Royal Parks and Gardens of London* (London, 1879), p. iv.

97 Ruskin, *The Poetry of Architecture*, p. 205; Watson, *Flowers and Gardens*, p. 148; Mrs [Margaret] Oliphant, *Miss Marjoribanks* (New York, 1867), p. 67; Robinson, *The Wild Garden*, p. 6.

4 The Geranium in the Window

 1 George Eliot, *Felix Holt, the Radical* (Oxford, 1981), pp. 6–7. Among many paintings of geraniumed cottage parlours are F. D. Hardy's *Early Sorrow* (1861) and *The Wedding Breakfast* (1871), W. H. Midwood's *Bedtime Stories* (1872) and William H. Snape's *A Cottage Home* (1891).

 2 Fyodor Dostoesvsky, *Poor Folk and Other Stories*, trans. David McDuff (London, 1988), p. 8.

 3 Flora Thompson, *Lark Rise* (1939), in *Lark Rise to Candleford* (London, 2008), p. 99; George Sturt, *Change in the Village* [1912] (Cambridge, 2010), p. 231.

 4 Lynn Hollens Lees, 'Urban Networks', in *The Cambridge Urban History of Britain*, vol. III: *1840–1950*, ed. Martin Daunton (Cambridge, 2000), p. 70.

 5 William Cowper, *The Task* (London, 1855), Book 4, ll. 757–88, pp. 163–4.

 6 Louis-Sébastien Mercier, 'Window-Boxes', in *Panorama of Paris*, trans. Helen Simpson, ed. Jeremy D. Popkin (University Park, PA, 1999), pp. 127–8.

 7 Charles Dickens, 'London Recreations', in *Sketches by Boz* (London, 1995), p. 119; *Jenny and her Geranium, or, The Prize Flower of a London Court* (London, 1841), p. 145.

 8 Thomas Fairchild, *The City Gardener* (London, 1722), p. 8.

 9 Waters, *The Garden in Victorian Literature*, p. 165; 'Flower Girls', in *Toilers in London; or Inquiries concerning Female Labour in the Metropolis*, ed. Margaret Harkness (London, 1889), p. 3.

10 Tom Taylor, 'Old Cottages', in *Birket Foster's Pictures of English Landscape with Pictures in Words by Tom Taylor* (London, 1863), p. 18; Peter Bailey, *Leisure and Class in Victorian England: Rational Recreations and the Context for Control, 1830–1885* (London, 1978).

11 Samuel Broome, 'On the Value of Town Gardens to the Poor', *Transactions of the National Association for the Promotion of Social Science* (London, 1859), p. 643.

12 Revd Samuel Hadden Parkes, *Window Gardens for the People, and Clean and Tidy Rooms; Being an Experiment to Improve the Lives of the London Poor* (London, 1864), p. 23.

13 *Jenny and her Geranium*, pp. 12–13.

14 Harriet Boultwood, *Dot's Scarlet Geranium* (London, 1890), p. 14.

15 'The Pot of Geranium', *Arthur's Home Magazine* (June 1868), pp. 339–40. Translated from German.

16 *Jenny and her Geranium*, p. 152. Parkes also talks of 'the germs of many social blessings'. *Window Gardens*, p. 77.

17 See James Winter, *Secure from Rash Assault* (Berkeley, CA, 1999), pp. 196–203.

18 Parkes, *Window Gardens*, p. 30.

19 Julia Matheson, '"A New Gleam of Social Sunshine": Window Garden Flower Shows for the Working Classes 1860–1875', *The London Gardener*, 9 (2003–4), p. 60. The original florists' flowers – including auriculas and carnations – had been supplemented by the pansy, dahlia, chrysanthemum and geranium. See Julia Matheson, 'Floricultural Societies and their Shows in the East End of London, 1860–1875', *The London Gardener*, 8 (2002–3), 26–33; Ruth Duthie, *Florists' Flowers and Societies* (Aylesbury, 1988); Wilkinson, *The Victorian Gardener*, ch. 6.

20 'Flower Shows in Towns for the Working Classes', *The Journal of Horticulture and Cottage Gardener* (30 April 1861), p. 75.

21 Geoffrey B.A.M. Finlayson, *The Seventh Earl of Shaftesbury, 1801–1885* (London, 1981), p. 76. See also Kenneth Hylson-Smith, *Evangelicals in the Church of England, 1734–1984* (Edinburgh, 1988), pp. 196–201.

22 'The Scarlet Geranium', *The Child's Companion* (1 September 1873), p. 138; Samuel Reynolds Hole, *The Six of Spades: A Book about the Garden and the Gardener* (Edinburgh, 1872), p. 72.

23 'Flower Shows in Towns for the Working Classes', pp. 75–6.

24 Walter H. Bosanquet, 'Flower Shows for the Poor in Town', *Journal of Horticulture and Cottage Gardener* (23 December 1862), p. 760; Parkes, *Window Gardens*, p. 30; 'Recreation', *Transactions of the National Association for the Promotion of Social Science, London Meeting 1862*, ed. George W. Hastings (London, 1862), p. 817.

25 'Bloomsbury Flower Show', *Journal of Horticulture and Cottage Gardener* (2 July 1861), p. 259; Parkes, *Window Gardens*, pp. 47, 45.

26 *The Story of a Geranium; or, The Queen of Morocco* (London, 1880), pp. 13, 44.

27 'Window Gardening', *The Lancet* (6 July 1867), p. 23. See also 'Exhibitions of Window-Gardened Plants', *Journal of Horticulture and Cottage Gardener* (9 July 1868), p. 27 and, on American ventures, Robert A. Woods and Albert J. Kennedy, *The Settlement Horizon* (New York, 1922), ch. 10.

28 Revd Samuel Hadden Parkes, *How to Grow a Plant; And Win a Prize* (London, 1865), pp. 3–4.

29 Anton Chekhov, 'A Peculiar Man', in *The Schoolmaster and Other Stories*, trans. Constance Garnett (London, 1921), p. 212.

30 George Eliot, 'Janet's Repentance', in *Scenes from a Clerical Life* (London, 1998), p. 211.

31 Thorburn, *Forty Years' Residence in America,* p. 94.

32 Parkes, *Window Gardens*, p. 12; George Godwin, *London Shadows* (London, 1854), p. 45; George Godwin, 'Overcrowding in London; and Some Remedial Measures', in *Transactions of the National Association for the Promotion of Social Science* (London, 1862), p. 594.

33 Quoted in Lynda Nead, *Victorian Babylon* (New Haven, CT, 2000), p. 94.

34 Shirley Hibberd, *The Town Garden* (London, 1855), pp. 6–7.

35 Charles Kingsley, *Glaucus* (Cambridge, 1855), p. 131.

36 Revd Samuel Hadden Parkes, *Flower Shows of Window Plants, for the Working Classes of London* (London, 1862), p. 5.

37 John Ruskin, *Modern Painters* (London, 1860), vol. V, p. 165.

38 Charles Kingsley, *Sanitary and Social Lectures and Essays* (London, 1880), p. 32.

39 Jane Jacobs, *The Death and Life of Great American Cities* (London, 1964), p. 101.

40 Kingsley, *Glaucus*, p. 131.

41 Christian Milne, 'Sent with a Flower-Pot, Begging a Slip of Geranium', *Simple Poems on Simple Subjects* (Aberdeen, 1805), p. 64; Mabel A. Clinton, 'Millie's Geranium', *Little Folks* (1892), pp. 51–53.

42 Emma Leslie, 'The Broken Geranium', *Kind Words*, 17 October 1867, p. 333.

43 'The Sulky Geranium', *Our Young Folks Weekly* (17 May 1873), p. 168.

44 Jennie Chappell, 'The Prize Geranium', in *Two Lilies and Other Stories* (London, 1888), pp. 55–64; Mary Russell Day, *John Marriot's Idol; or, The Scarlet Geranium* (London, 1888), pp. 55, 60.

45 For example, in *Ethics for Children*, ed. E. C. Cabot (Boston, MA, 1910).

46 Edward Bulwer Lytton, *The Caxtons* (London, 1949), vol. I, pp. 17–22.

47 George Eliot, *Middlemarch* (Oxford, 2008), p. 84.

48 Quoted in F. W. Burbidge, *Domestic Floriculture: Window-gardening and Floral Decoration* (Edinburgh, 1874), p. 6.

49 Louisa May Alcott, *Little Women* (Oxford, 2008), p. 48; *The Floral Knitting Book , or, The Art of Knitting Imitations of Natural Flowers, Invented by a Lady* (London, 1860), pp. 21–2, 26–7. See also Joan Morgan and Alison Richards, *A Paradise out of a Common Field: The Pleasures and Plenty of the Victorian Garden* (London, 1990), pp. 57, 64–6, 196–7.

50 Leigh Hunt, 'Love-letters Made of Flowers', *The Poetical Works* (Boston, MA, 1863), vol. II, p. 169.

51 Anna Christian Burke, *The Illustrated Language of Flowers* (London, 1856), p. 26. For a 'combined vocabulary' drawn from several books, see Beverly Seaton, *The Language of Flowers* (Charlottesville, VA, 1995), pp. 178–9.

52 Charlotte M. Yonge, *The Young Step-mother* (London, 1861), p. 145.

53 Charles Dickens, *The Pickwick Papers* (Oxford, 1986), p. 535; Dickens, *Dombey and Son*, p. 562.

54 Mrs. C. W. Earle, *Pot-pourri from a Surrey Garden* [1897] (Chichester, 2004), p. 212.

55 Thomas Hood, *Selected Poems*, ed. Joy Flint (Manchester, 1992), p. 105.

56 Alcott, *Little Women*, p. 48.

57 *Jenny and Her Geranium*, p. 13.
58 'Her One Treasure', *Our Darlings* (1 June 1889), p. 254; Parkes, *Window Gardens*, p. 50.
59 James J. Gebhard, Introduction to A. F. Veltman, *Selected Stories*, trans. Gebhard (Evanston, IL, 1998), p. 8.
60 Veltman, 'Travel Impressions and, among Other Things, a Pot of Geraniums' in *Selected Stories*, pp. 63–94.
61 *Jenny and Her Geranium*, p. 68.
62 Watson, *Flowers and Gardens*, p. 140.
63 Charlotte S. M. Barnes, 'The Dead Geranium', *The Churchman's Magazine*, 8 (1845), p. 7.
64 Dickens, *David Copperfield*, pp. 394–5, 480–82, 805.
65 Elizabeth Gaskell, *Mary Barton* (Oxford, 2006), pp. 5–6, 14–15, 95.
66 Charlotte Latour, *Le Langage des Fleurs* (1819), p. 175. My translation.
67 Folly is given by Robert Tyas, *The Language of Flowers* (London, 1868), p. 180; stupidity by Frederic Schoberl, *The Language of Flowers* (Philadelphia, 1848), pp. 216–17, and Henrietta Dumont, *The Language of Flowers* (Philadelphia, 1852), p. 147. For comfort, see Burke, *The Illustrated Language of Flowers*, p. 26.
68 Robert Browning, *The Major Works* (Oxford, 1997), pp. 59, 170.
69 Thomas Hardy, *Far from the Madding Crowd* (Oxford, 2002), pp. 11–12.
70 Stephen Regan, 'The Darkening Pastoral', in *A Companion to Thomas Hardy*, ed. Keith Wilson (Oxford, 2009), p. 249.
71 Gustave Flaubert, *Madame Bovary*, trans. Geoffrey Wall (London, 1992), pp. 31, 55; Laurie Lee, 'Day of These Days', in *The Bloom of Candles* (London, 1947), p. 10.
72 Dostoevsky, *Crime and Punishment*, trans. Jessie Coulson (Oxford, 2008), p. 5.
73 André Breton, *Manifestos of Surrealism*, trans. Richard Seaver and Helen S. Lane (Ann Arbor, MI, 1969), pp. 7–8.
74 There is a discrepancy in her age. On one page, we're told she's fourteen and on another that she is ten. Fyodor Dostoevsky, *The Devils*, trans. Michael R. Katz (Oxford, 1999), pp. 268, 461, 472. Dostoevsky's publisher thought this chapter too shocking to print and it remained unpublished during his lifetime.
75 Dostoevsky, *The Devils*, pp. 464, 467, 472.

5 Brief Fall, then Inexorable Rise

1 John Gray, *Silverpoints* (London, 1893), p. xx; Michael Frayn, *Alphabetical Order* (1977), Act 2 (London, 2009), p. 46.
2 'The Point of View', *Scribner's Magazine*, LVI/1 (1914), p. 130.
3 Henry James, *The Spoils of Poynton* (Oxford, 2000), p. 35.
4 Willa Cather, 'The Novel Démeublé' in *Not Under Forty* (New York, 1936), p. 47.
5 Catherine Harwood, *Potted History* (London, 2007), pp. 156–7, 159–60.
6 H. N. Tomlinson, 'The "Heart's Desire"', *The Owl*, 2 (1919), p. 38.

7 'The Point of View', p. 130.

8 Ronald Richings, 'The House of Blood', *Coterie*, nos. 6/7 (1920), pp. 77–85.

9 Alice Martineau, *The Secrets of Many Gardens* (London, 1924), p. 70.

10 Jenny Uglow, *A Little History of British Gardening* (London, 2004), p. 255.

11 Virginia Woolf, *Mrs Dalloway* (London, 1992), pp. 28, 92, 94, 97, 98, 20.

12 'Celebrating 90 Years of Geranium Day', at www.glfb.org.uk, last accessed 28 May 2012.

13 Louis MacNeice, *Collected Poems* (London, 2007), pp. 95–6; 141–3.

14 Aldous Huxley, *Brave New World* (London, 1994), p. 43; David Gascoyne, *Collected Poems* (Oxford, 1988), p. 25.

15 T. S. Eliot, *The Complete Poems and Plays* (London, 1969), p. 24; Jules Laforgue, *Poems*, trans. Peter Dale (London, 1986), p. 409. Laforgue, said Eliot, 'made it impossible for anyone else to talk about geraniums'. *The Letters of T. S. Eliot*, vol. II: *1923–1925* (London, 2009), p. 241. See also T. S. Eliot, *Inventions of the March Hare, Poems 1909–1917* (London, 1996), p. 142.

16 T. S. Eliot, 'The Metaphysical Poets', *Selected Prose* (London, 1975), pp. 65–6.

17 See Uldis Ports, 'Geraniums vs. Smokestacks: San Diego's Mayoralty Campaign of 1917', *The Journal of San Diego History*, XXI/3 (Summer 1975), pp. 50–56.

18 Eliot, *The Complete Poems and Plays*, p. 25.

19 Sylvia Plath, 'Leaving Early', *Collected Poems* (London, 2002), p. 145. Zonals are sometimes known in America as Fish Geraniums. Louise Beebe Wilder, *The Fragrant Garden* (New York, 1974), p. 184.

20 Eliot, *Inventions of the March Hare*, pp. 23–4.

21 Arthur Miller, *Focus* (1945) (London, 1958), p. 70. Storm Jameson, *A Day Off* (London, 1933), p. 11; Storm Jameson, *The Moon is Making* (London, 1937), pp. 320–21; Flannery O'Connor, 'The Geranium', *Collected Stories* (London, 1990), pp. 7, 14. Thanks to Anna Kanakova for the Jameson references.

22 Regina Spektor, 'Back of a Truck', *11:11* (2001); A. M. Homes, *Music for Torching* (London, 1999), pp. 201, 84; William Kotzwinkle, *E.T. The Extra-Terrestrial* (New York, 1982), pp. 92–3.

23 Also by Cézanne, see *Geranium and Larkspur in a Delft Vase* (1873), *Pots of Geraniums* (1888), and *Still Life with Fruit and Geraniums* (1894), and, by Matisse, *Still Life with a Geranium* (1906) and *Spanish Still-life* (1910–11).

24 The text was taken from the script of D. W. Griffith's film *Intolerance* (1916).

25 In 1865 La Muette greenhouses produced 870,000 bedding plants for Paris's gardens and parks. Clare A. P. Willesdon, *Impressionist Gardens* (London, 2010), p. 23.

26 Hassam's *Geraniums* features his wife Maude in the doorway of their rented house in Villiers-le-Bel, near Paris. Willesdon, *Impressionist Gardens* p. 67, 153.

27 Clare A. P. Willesdon, *In the Gardens of Impressionism* (New York, 2004), p. 169.

28 Derek Jarman, *Chroma* (London, 1994), p. 33. See also Anthea Callen, *The Art of Impressionism* (New Haven, CT, 2000), pp. 73–5.

29 See Monet's *Terrace at Sainte-Adresse* (1867).
30 The others are *Camille in the Garden with Jean and his Nurse* (1873) and *The Luncheon* (1873), which formed the focal point of the 1876 Impressionist Exhibition. Willesdon, *In the Gardens*, p. 131.
31 Mary Mathews Gedo, *Monet and his Muse: Camille Monet in the Artist's Life* (Chicago, 2010), pp. 130–33; Joel Isaacson, *Claude Monet, Observation and Reflection* (Oxford, 1978), p. 208; Willesdon, *In the Gardens*, p. 148.
32 Gedo, *Monet and his Muse*, p. 133.
33 'O Glaros' ('The Seagull'), music by Manos Hadjidakis and lyrics by Alekos Sakellarios, from the 1961 film *I Aliki sto naftiko* (*Aliki in the Navy*). Translation from the Greek by Ali Smith.
34 Willesdon, *In the Gardens*, p. 18.
35 D. H. Lawrence, 'Education of the People', in *Reflections on the Death of a Porcupine and Other Essays*, ed. Michael Herbert (Cambridge, 1988), p. 153.
36 D. H. Lawrence, 'Red Geranium and Godly Mignonette', *Complete Poems* (London, 1972), vol. II, p. 690.
37 D. H. Lawrence, *Sea and Sardinia* (Cambridge, 1997), p. 120; D. H. Lawrence, *Twilight in Italy* (Cambridge, 2002), p. 123.
38 D. H. Lawrence, *The Rainbow* (London, 2007), p. 346.
39 *The Journal of Katherine Mansfield*, ed. J. Middleton Murray (London, 1954), p. 157.
40 Ibid., p. 9; D. H. Lawrence, *The Letters*, vol. V: *1924–27*, ed. James T. Boulton and Lindeth Vasey (Cambridge, 1989), p. 376; Lawrence, 'Butterfly', *Complete Poems*, vol. II, p. 696.
41 Leigh Hunt, *The Autobiography* (Boston, MA, 1870), p. 324.
42 Joanna Trollope, *A Spanish Lover* (London, 2010), p. 274; John Mortimer, *Summer's Lease* (London, 1988), p. 46.
43 Gertrude Jekyll, 'Colour in the Flower Garden', in William Robinson, *The English Flower Garden* (London, 1998), p. 121; Willesdon, *In the Gardens*, p. 25.
44 Walter P. Wright, *The Perfect Garden* (London, 1908), p. 22.
45 Robinson, *The English Flower Garden*, p. 20; Gertrude Jekyll, *Wood and Garden* [1899] (Cambridge, 2011), p. 264, 210.
46 Judith B. Tankard and Martin A. Wood, *Gertude Jekyll at Munstead Wood* (Stroud, 1996), p. 98.
47 Jekyll, 'Colour in the Flower Garden', p. 121.
48 Jekyll, *Wood and Garden*, pp. 266–8. In turn-of-the-century England, every mention of a scarlet geranium was prefaced 'I do not despise'. See, for example, Earle, *Pot-pourri from a Surrey Garden*, p. 133.
49 Jekyll, *Wood and Garden*, p. 268.
50 Her comment that artists 'laugh at' the colour 'laws' produced by chemists and decorators is presumably a dig at Chevreul. Jekyll, 'Colour in the Flower Garden', pp. 120–21.
51 In other garden plans, she included red antirrhinums and perennial kniphofias and penstemons. Richard Bisgrove, *The Gardens of Gertrude Jekyll* (Berkeley, CA, 1992), p. 185; Tankard and Wood, *Gertrude Jekyll at Munstead Wood*, p. 23.

52 'My eye has had too much tender tutoring', she wrote, 'to endure the popular "Henry Jacoby" – a colour that, for all its violence, has a harsh dullness that I find displeasing.' Gertrude Jekyll, *Colour Schemes for the Flower Garden* [1914] (London, 1988), pp. 71–2; 147–8; 101–2. Jekyll, *Wood and Garden*, p. 267.

53 Tankard and Wood, *Gertrude Jekyll at Munstead Wood*, p. 24.

54 Joris-Karl Huysmans, *Against Nature*, trans. Robert Baldick (London, 2003), pp. 22, 83.

55 Marcel Proust, *The Way by Swann's* (1913), trans. Lydia Davis (London, 2003), p. 178; Laforgue, *Poems*, p. 199.

56 Carson McCullers, *The Member of the Wedding* (London, 2001), p. 185; Albert Camus, *The Stranger*, trans. Matthew Ward (New York, 1988), p. 18; Virginia Woolf, *To the Lighthouse* (Oxford, 2006), pp. 37, 30–31.

57 Walter Benjamin, 'Berlin Childhood around 1900 (final version)', in *Selected Writings*, vol. III: *1935–1938* (Cambridge, MA, 2002), p. 346.

58 Nella Larsen, *Passing* (1929) (New York, 2002), p. 37.

59 Maude E. Miner, *Slavery of Prostitution: A Plea for Emancipation* (New York, 1916), p. 164.

60 Harper Lee, *To Kill a Mockingbird* [1960] (London, 2010), pp. 188, 197.

61 [M.E. Braddon] *Birds of Prey* (London, 1867), 3 vols, vol. I, pp. 2–3, 5–6.

62 Frederick Wertham, *A Sign for Cain* (New York, 1966), ch. 9, 'The Geranium in the Window'.

63 Walker Percy, *The Thanatos Syndrome* (New York, 1987), pp. 274–8.

64 Kurt Gerstein, 'Deathwatch at Bełżec', in *A Holocaust Reader*, ed. Lucy S. Dawidowicz (New York, 1976), pp. 107–8.

65 Rodgers and Hammerstein, 'Geraniums in the Winder', *Carousel* (1945). The song doesn't feature in the film adaptation of 1956.

66 Ann Petry, *The Street* (London, 1947), p. 25.

67 William H. Young and Nancy K. Young, *The 1950s* (Westport, CT, 2004), p. 97.

68 John Cross, *The Book of the Geranium* (London, 1951), pp. 113–14.

69 'The London Geranium', *The Times*, 21 September 1950, p. 5; Wilkinson, *The Passion for Pelargoniums*, p. 223. See also 'How "Gustav Emich" was Introduced', *The Times* (26 September 1950), p. 4. In the 1970s 'Gustav Emich' was replaced by the 'Sprinter' range. Janet James, 'Cultivation and Sales of *Pelargonium* Plants for Ornamental Use in the UK and Worldwide', in *Geranium and Pelargonium*, ed. Maria Lis-Balchin (London, 2002), p. 81.

70 It was later renamed the British Pelargonium and Geranium Society. Cross's model was the American Pelargonium Society which ran from 1940 to 1942. The (US-based) International Pelargonium Society was founded in 1950 (reformed as the International Geranium Society in 1953). Thanks to Faye Brawner, President of the International Geranium Society, for information on the American scene. Cross, *The Book of the Geranium*, pp. 75, 112–13.

71 Clifford thought they resembled 'Angeline', a cultivar described by Sweet. The modern hybrids were created by Arthur Langley-Smith.

Anne Wilkinson, *The Passion for Pelargoniums* (Stroud, 2007), pp. 220–21; Faye Brawner, *Geraniums: The Complete Encyclopedia* (New York, 2003), pp. 90, 121.

72 For much more detail, see Brawner, *Geraniums* and Key, *1001 Pelargoniums*.

73 See www.geraniaceae-group.org/developing_zonartic.html and www.prize-pelargoniums.com.

74 Elizabeth Kent, *Flora Domestica* (London, 1823), p. 145. The 2008 *International Register and Checklist of Pelargonium Cultivars* had over 15,000 entries; a 2011 Addendum listed a further 1,200.

75 F2 seed – produced by cross- or self-pollinating F1 plants – results in more variable stock but is much cheaper to produce.

76 Wilkinson, *The Passion for Pelargoniums*, pp. 234–5; James, 'Cultivation and sales', pp. 81–2.

77 Telephone interview with Steve Waters of Syngenta, 20 May 2010.

78 Nona Koivula, 'History of the Flower Seed Industry', in *Flower Seeds: Biology and Technology*, ed. M. B. McDonald and F. Y. Kwong (Cambridge, MA, 2005), p. 24.

79 'Bedding Plants', University of Kentucky Agricultural College Information Sheet, at www.uky.edu, last accessed 28 May 2012; James, 'Cultivation and Sales', p. 90.

80 A. M. Homes, 'The Bullet Catcher', *The Safety of Objects* (London, 1990), p. 97.

81 Cross, *The Book of the Geranium*, p. 69.

82 Cicely Mary Barker, *A Flower Fairies Treasury* (London, 1997), p. 92. See also Martin Postle's discussion in *Art of the Garden*, eds. Nicholas Alfrey, Stephen Daniels and Martin Postle (London, 2004), pp. 110–11.

83 Jeanette Oke, *The Red Geranium* (Minneapolis, 1995), p. 67; Kate Millett, *Mother Millett* (London, 2002), p. 127.

84 Linda Newbery, *Lob* (Oxford, 2010), p. 179.

85 Barbara Johnson, *Daily Splashes of Joy* (Nashville, TN, 2000), entry for 23 January. Johnson's other books include *Stick a Geranium in Your Hat and Be Happy!* and *Plant a Geranium in Your Cranium*.

86 *The Collected Letters of Katherine Mansfield*, vol. V: *1922–1923*, ed. Vincent O'Sullivan and Margaret Scott (Oxford, 2008), p. 124.

87 Clement Wood, 'Rose-Geranium', *Glad of Earth* (New York, 1917), p. 15; Ivan Turgenev, 'Asya', in *First Love and Other Stories*, trans. Richard Freeborn (Oxford, 2008), p. 143.

88 Marcel Proust, *By Way of Saint-Beuve*, trans. Sylvia Townsend Warner (London, 1958), p. 17.

89 Marcel Proust, *The Captive*, trans. Scott Moncrieff, Terence Kilmartin and D. J. Enright (London, 2000), p. 428.

90 Juan Francisco Manzano, *The Autobiography of a Slave*, trans. Evelyn Picon Garfield and Ivan A. Schulman (Detroit, 1996), pp. 89, 91.

91 See Frédéric-Emmanuel Demarne, '"Rose-scented Geranium": A *Pelargonium* Grown for the Perfume Industry', in *Geranium and Pelargonium*, ed. Lis-Balchin.

92 The Sicilian cosmetics company Ortigia uses oil derived from the mint-scented *P. tomentosum.*

93 Maria Lis-Balchin, 'Geranium Essential Oil', in *Geranium and Pelargonium,* ed. Lis-Balchin, p. 189.

94 Demarne, '"Rose-scented Geranium"', p. 200; Christine A. Williams and Jeffrey B. Harborne, 'Phytochemistry of the Genus *Pelargonium*', in *Geranium and Pelargonium,* ed. Lis-Balchin, p. 99.

95 For ideas on cooking and making cosmetics with scented pelargoniums, see Susan Conder, *The Complete Geranium* (New York, 1992), ch. 5, and *Pelargoniums: A Herb Society of America Guide* (Kirtland, OH, 2006), pp. 21–48.

96 Stephen Hart and Maria Lis-Balchin, 'Pharmacology of Pelargonium Essential Oils and Extracts *in vitro* and *in vivo*', in *Geranium and Pelargonium,* ed. Lis-Balchin, p. 116.

97 Elspeth Thompson, *The London Gardener* (London, 2006), p. 111; Marina Christopher, *Late Summer Flowers* (London, 2006), p. 160.

98 F. B. Smith, *The Retreat of Tuberculosis, 1850–1950* (London, 1988), p. 156. For a full account, see S.W.B. Newsom, 'Stevens' Cure: A Secret Remedy', *Journal of the Royal Society of Medicine,* 95 (September 2002), 463–67.

99 David Ellis, *D. H. Lawrence: Dying Game, 1922–1930* (Cambridge, 1998), p. 379. *The Letters of D. H. Lawrence,* vol. VI, eds James T. Boulton, Margaret H. Boulton and Gerald M. Lacy (Cambridge, 1991), p. 350. See also, pp. 226, 361, 367, 413.

100 Gail Patrick and John Hickner, 'This Obscure Herb Works for the Common Cold', *The Journal of Family Practice,* LVII/3 (March 2008), 157–60.

101 A. Timmer, J. Günther, G. Rücker, E. Motschall, G. Antes, W. V. Kern, 'Pelargonium sidoides extract for acute respiratory tract infections', *Cochrane Database of Systematic Reviews* (2008), Issue 3. Art. No.: CD006323. DOI: 10.1002/14651858.CD006323.pub2.

Postscript

1 D. H. Lawrence, *Complete Poems* (London, 1972), vol. II, p. 690; A. A. Milne, *When We Were Very Young* (London, 2007), p. 67.

2 Derek Jarman, *Chroma* (London, 1994), pp. 31–3.

3 *The Collected Letters of Katherine Mansfield,* vol. IV: *1920–1921,* ed. Vincent O'Sullivan and Margaret Scott (Oxford, 1996), p. 312. The angel's visit to previously barren Sarah is an allusion to Genesis 18:1–15.

4 *The Collected Letters of Katherine Mansfield,* vol. IV, pp. 316–317.

5 Another version of the scene can be found in August Macke's *Geraniums Before Blue Mountain* (1911), on show at the Milwaukee Museum of Art. Macke's painting is different, somehow both vivid and cosy: mountains, houses and geraniums coexist companionably in a kind of cartoon universe.

Further Reading

Alfrey, Nicholas, Stephen Daniels and Martin Postle, eds, *Art of the Garden: The Garden in British Art, 1800 to the Present Day* (London, 2004)
Brawner, Faye, *Geraniums: The Complete Encyclopedia* (New York, 2003)
Conder, Susan, *The Complete Geranium: Cultivation, Cooking and Crafts* (New York, 1992)
Elliott, Brent, *Victorian Gardens* (Portland, OR, 1986)
Fraser, Mike, and Liz Fraser, *The Smallest Kingdom: Plants and Plant Collectors at the Cape of Good Hope* (London, 2011)
Harwood, Catherine, *Potted History: The Story of Plants in the Home* (London, 2007)
Key, Hazel, *1001 Pelargoniums* (London, 2003)
Laird, Mark, and Alicia Weisberg-Roberts, eds, *Mrs Delany and her Circle* (New Haven, CT, 2009)
Lis-Balchin, Maria, ed., *Geranium and Pelargonium* (London, 2002)
Miller, Diana, *Pelargoniums* (London, 1996)
Joan Morgan and Alison Richards, *A Paradise out of a Common Field: The Pleasures and Plenty of the Victorian Garden* (London, 1990)
Saunders, Gill, *Picturing Plants* (Berkeley, CA, 1995)
Uglow, Jenny, *A Little History of British Gardening* (London, 2004)
Walt, J.J.A. van der, and P. J. Vorster, with illustrations by Ellaphie Ward-Hilhorst, *Pelargoniums of Southern Africa*, 3 volumes (1977–1988)
Wilkinson, Anne, *The Passion for Pelargoniums* (Stroud, 2007)
Willesdon, Clare A. P., *In the Gardens of Impressionism* (New York, 2004)

Associations and Websites

BOTANICUS (MISSOURI BOTANICAL GARDEN)
www.botanicus.org

CUSTODIANS OF RARE AND ENDANGERED WILDFLOWERS PROGRAMME
www.sanbi.org/programmes/threats/custodians-rare-and-endangered-wild-
flowers-crew-programme

THE GERANIACEAE GROUP
www.geraniaceae-group.org

GERANIUMS ONLINE
www.geraniumsonline.com

THE INTERNATIONAL GERANIUM SOCIETY
www.internationalgeraniumsociety.com

THE PELARGONIUM AND GERANIUM SOCIETY
www.thepags.org.uk

PELARGONIUMS: A HERB SOCIETY OF AMERICA GUIDE (2006)
www.herbsociety.org/factsheets/Pelargonium%20Guide.pdf

PLANTS OF SOUTHERN AFRICA
http://posa.sanbi.org/searchspp.php

THE RED LIST OF SOUTH AFRICAN PLANTS 2011
http://redlist.sanbi.org

SOUTH AFRICAN NATIONAL BIODIVERSITY INSTITUTE
www.sanbi.org

Acknowledgements

In finding illustrations I have depended on the help and generosity of many people and organizations. I'd particularly like to thank:

Max Antheunisse at plantillustrations.org; Alyssa Anzalone at True Botanica; Virginia Apuzzo at Cambridge University Library Imaging Department; Claudio Bacinello; Faye Brawner, President of the International Geranium Society; Gillian Condy at the National Herbarium, South African National Biodiversity Institute; Susan Goldswain at Quarry Lake Inn; Jarvis Gurr at English Heritage; Rikki Nyman at Mid Century Home Style; Lynn Parker at the Royal Botanical Gardens, Kew; Steve Waters, Andrew Coker and Jodie Champion at Syngenta; and Sharon Willoughby at the Royal Botanical Gardens, Melbourne. Most generous of all has been John Manning at the Kirstenbosch Research Centre in South Africa, who supplied me with a wonderful selection of his field photographs.

I am also very grateful to all the friends and relations who gave me geraniums and helped me with geraniana: especially, Edward Allen, Rosemary Ashton, Matt Beaumont, Ada Boddy, Janet Boddy, Tracy Bohan, Melissa Calaresu, David Colquhoun, Greg Dart, Mark Ford, Heather Glen, Tag Gronberg, Judith Hawley, Beth Housdon, Matt Ingelby, Anna Kanakova, Patrick Kennedy, Alison Light, Tôbi Megchild, Charlotte Mitchell, Rajeswari Mohan, Lynda Nead, Barbara Placido, Vidya Ravi, Ali Smith, Tom Ue, and Sarah Wood. Andrew Boddy provided invaluable help, right to the end. But David Trotter, as always, deserves the biggest thanks.

Parts of this book draw on two previously published essays: 'Potting', in *Restless Cities*, ed. Matthew Beaumont and Gregory Dart (London, 2010), pp. 212–31; and 'Bloomsbury in Bloom', the UCL Bloomsbury Project (2010): www.ucl.ac. uk/bloomsbury-project.

Photo Acknowledgements

The author and publishers wish to express their thanks to the below sources of illustrative material and/or permission to reproduce it. (Some information not placed in the captions for reasons of brevity is also given below.)

Photograph by Max Antheunisse, 2003: p. 22 (foot); photo courtesy of the Ashmolean Museum Picture Library, Oxford (presented to the Ruskin Drawing School, University of Oxford, 1875): p. 93; photos by the author: pp. 24, 72, 87 (top), 102, 156, 157, 166, 177 (foot); photo Claudio Bacinello: p. 57; Badminton House, Gloucestershire: p. 45; from *Belle assemblée, being Bell's Court and Fashionable Magazine: addressed particularly to the ladies*, XX / 129 (December 1819): p. 95; photo Andrew Boddy: p. 86; from Jacob Breyne, *Exoticarum aliarumque minus cogitarum Plantarum Centuria Prima, cum figuris æneis [. . .] elaboratis* (Danzig, 1678): p. 39; photos © The Bridgeman Art Library: p. 101 (foot), 141, 142; British Museum, London: p. 48; photos © The Trustees of the British Museum, London: pp. 48, 69; from E. Adveno Brooke, *The Gardens of England* (London, 1857): p. 82; from *Chain Store Age* (January 1949): p. 161; from the Chicago *Daily News* (2 June 1964): p. 159; photograph from the *Chicago Sun-Times* (30 September 1951) by Mel Larson: p. 167; from Jacques-Phillipe Cornut, *Canadensium plantarum, aliarumque nondum editarum historia: cui adiectum est ad cacem enchiridion botanicum Parisiense, continens indicem plantarum* (Paris, 1635): p. 25; photo © *Country Life*: p. 155; from *The Cries of London, as they are daily exhibited in the street* (London, 1799): p. 103; from *Curtis's Magazine* no. 1718 (1 April, 1815): p. 51; from Johann Jakob Dillenius, *Hortus Elthamensis seu plantarum rariorum icones et nomina [. . .] descriptarum Elthamenia in Cantio in horto viri ornatissimi atque praestantissimi Jacobi Sherard* (London, 1732): p. 43 (top); photo © Edifice / The Bridgeman Art Library: p. 9; photo Antony Edwards / IC Images Ltd: p. 149; from John Edwards, *A Collection of Flowers, drawn after Nature and Disposed in an Ornamental and Picturesque Manner* (London, 1795): p. 52; photo © English Heritage Photo Library: p. 53 (top); from *Familiar Garden Flowers figured by F. Edward Hulme, and described by Shirley Hibberd* (London, 1880): p. 5; Fitzwilliam Museum, Cambridge (Broughton Collection – photo © Fitzwilliam Museum): p. 50; from *The Floral Magazine: comprising Figures and Descriptions of Popular Garden Flowers*: pp. 90 (vol. II, 1862), 91 (vol. VII, 1868); from *The Floral World and Garden*

Guide, vol. VII (July 1864): p. b87 (foot); courtesy of the Florence Griswold Museum, Old Lyme, Connecticut (photo © Christie's Images / The Bridgeman Art Library): pp. 64–5; from *Flower Fairies of the Garden* (London, 1944): p. 170; first published in *Flowering Plants of Africa* (South African National Biodiversity Institute), vol. 50 (Cape Town, 1989): p. 21; reproduced with permission of Mrs Susan Goldswain: p. 21; from Robert Furber, *The Twelve Months of Flowers (in 13 illuminated plates, including the title-page* (London, 1730): p. 46; Geffrye Museum, London (photo © Geffrye Museum / The Bridgeman Art Library): p. 124; from *The Graphic*: pp. 81 (issue 27, 4 June 1870), 112 (issue 780, 8 November 1884); from Félix-Edouard Guérin-Méneville, ed., *Dictionnaire pittoresque d'histoire naturelle et des phénomènes de la nature*, VII (Paris, 1833–[40]): p. 74; from Aylwin Guilmant, *England of One Hundred Years Ago* (Stroud, 1992): p. 101 (top); © David Henderson / Science Photo Library: p. 10; digital specimen images at the Herbarium Berolinense, published on the Internet http://ww2.bgbm.org/herbarium/ (Barcode: B -W 12463 -01 0/ImageId: 233330), accessed 3 Sept 2012 – © Botanic Garden and Botanical Museum Berlin-Dahlem, Freie Universität Berlin: p. 41; from Henry Hoare, *Spade Work: Or, How to Start a Flower Garden* (London, 1902): p. 131; from *Hortus Botanicus Amsterdans* (Amsterdam, 1690): p. 28; The Hunterian Museum and Art Gallery, University of Glasgow (photo © The Hunterian Museum and Art Gallery): p. 144; Hyde Collection, Glens Falls, New York (photo Michael Fredericks): p. 147; from the *Illustrated London News* (26 April 1873): pp. 104–5; from *L'Industrie des Parfums à Grasse*, promotional album for the Paris Exposition Universelle, 1900: p. 177 (top); from *Jenny and Her Geranium; or, The Prize Flower of a London Court* (London, 1869): p. 108; photo © Geoff Kidd / Science Photo Library: p. 168; from Charles-Louis L'Héritier, *Geraniologia, seu Erodii, pelargonii, geranii, monsoniae et grieli historia iconibus illustrata* (Paris, 1787–8): p. 40; Laing Art Gallery, Newcastle upon Tyne (photo © Tyne & Wear Archives & Museums / The Bridgeman Art Library): p. 100; photo © Lefevre Fine Art Ltd, London / The Bridgeman Art Library: p. 142; from *Little Folks: A Magazine for the Young*, no. 27: p. 110; photographs by John Manning: pp. 22 (top), 23, 26, 29; from John Martyn, *Historia Plantarum Rariorum*, 5 vols (London, 1728–37): p. 43 (foot); courtesy of *Mid-Century Home Style*: p. 162; from Abraham Munting, *Phytographia Curiosa: exhibens arborum, fruticum, herbarum & florum icones, ducentis et quadraginta quinque tabulis ad vivum delineatis ac artificiosissime æri incisis; varias earum denominationes, Latinas, Gallicas, Italicas, Germanicas aliasque [. . .] desumptas / collegit & adjecit Franciscus Kiggelaer* (Utrecht, 1702): p. 44; Musée d'Orsay, Paris: p. 146; courtesy of the Museo Civico e Gipsoteco Bistolfi, Casale Monferrato: pp. 180–81; courtesy of the National Gallery of Art, Washington, DC: pp. 59, 143 (Chester Dale Collection); photo © Natural History Museum, London (The *Endeavour* Botanical Illustrations): p. 34; from Linda Newbery, *Lob* (Oxford, 2010): p. 171; from John Parkinson, *Theatrum Botanicum, The Theater of Plantes, or an Universall and Compleate Herball* (London, 1640): p. 38; private collections: pp. 101 (foot), 141, 142, 148; private collection / Ken Welsh / The Bridgeman Art Library: p. 96; from Humphry Repton, *Fragments on the Theory and Practice of Landscape Gardening, including some remarks on Grecian and Gothic Architecture* (London, 1816): p. 75; photo © Rosenfeld Images Ltd/Science Photo Library:

p. 169; courtesy of the Royal Botanic Gardens, Kew: p. 19; © Steve G. Schmeissner / Science Photo Library: p. 17; photo © Science Photo Library: p. 174; photo Science and Society Picture Library / Bridgeman Art Library: p. 152; photos © The Stapleton Collection / The Bridgeman Art Library: pp. 103, 177 (top); State Tretyakov Gallery, Moscow (image © Lebrecht Music & Arts): p. 145; from *The Story of a Geranium; or, The Queen of Morocco* (London, 1880): p. 113; from Robert Sweet, *Geraniaceae: the natural order of gerania: illustrated by coloured figures and descriptions: comprising the numerous and beautiful mule-varieties cultivated in the gardens of Great Britain, with directions for their treatment*, vol. I (London, 1820–22): pp. 70, 73; photo © True Botanica Company: p. 178; photo courtesy of the University Library of the University of Amsterdam (Special Collections Department): p. 28; Victoria and Albert Museum, London (photo © Victoria and Albert Museum): p. 53 (foot); photo Peter Willi / The Bridgeman Art Library: p. 148; photo Sharon Willoughby (courtesy thetomatogrower.wordpress.com): p. 94; photo © Worthing Museum and Art Gallery, Sussex / The Bridgeman Art Library: p. 132.

Index